Galactic Shamanism
the Star-Stone Ones

by
Mary Saint-Marie/ Sheoekah

a story that reflects and inspires our collective passage into the "once upon a non-time..."

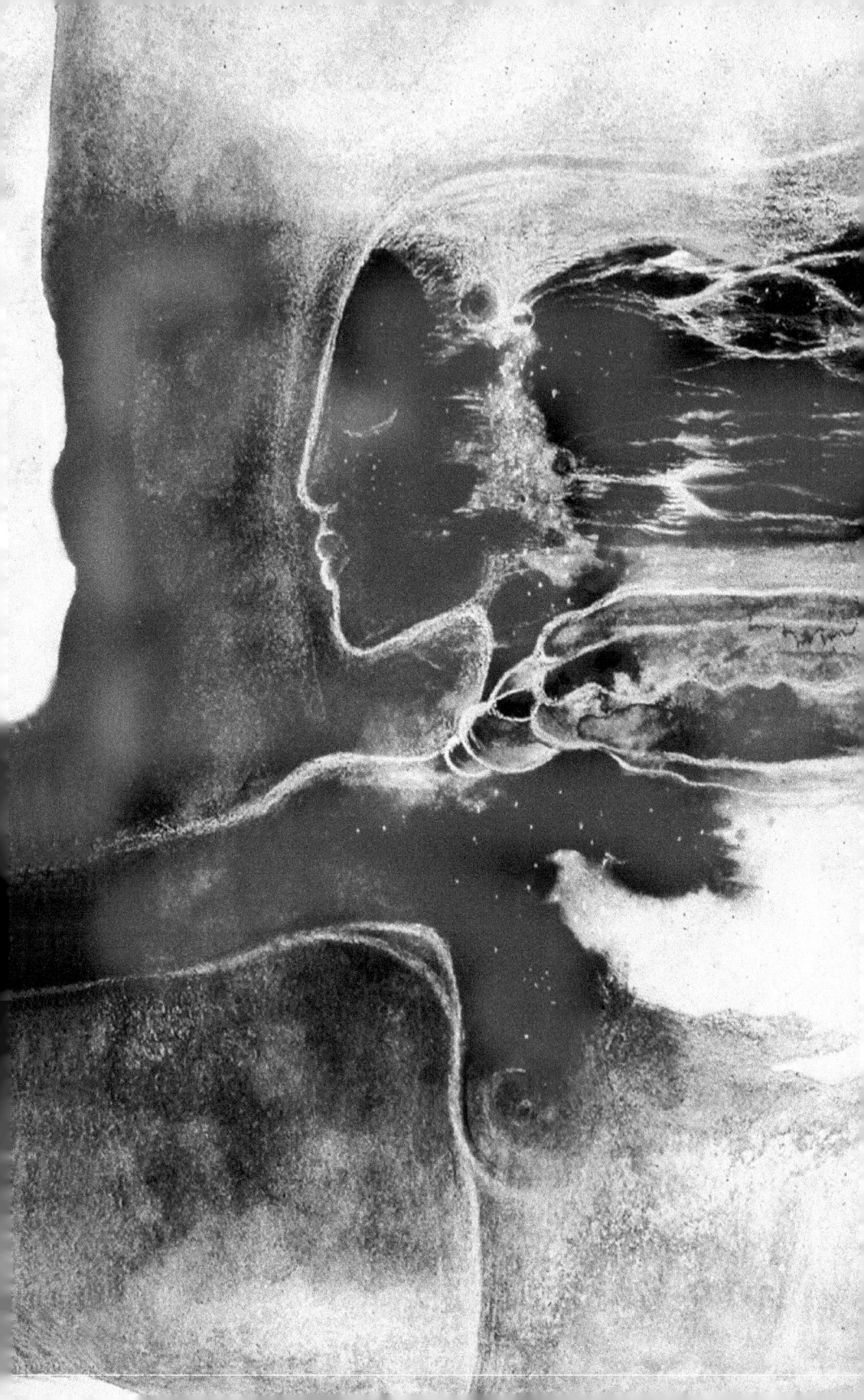

Shards of HER-story have been gathered
from the Archetypal Realm Templates.
This seemingly personal story
of journeys into inner realms
unveils an inspiring Impersonal Odyssey
of the Soul's Remembering
happening
unto these very times.

Second Edition, Revised 2016
© 1995, 2016 Mary Saint-Marie / Sheoekah. All Rights Reserved.

No part of this book may be reproduced, stored in a retrieval system, or transmitted by any means without the written permission of the author.

Published by Ancient Beauty Studio, www.marysaintmarie.com

ISBN: 978-0-615-39139-7 (sc)

All artwork by Mary Saint-Marie

Cover Art: *Star-Stone Essence-SHE*

Titlepage Art: *Journey-SHE…from the Stars unto the Stones*

Author Photos by Rebecca Allen

Credit for NASA Public Domain Image of M35: Atlas Image obtained as part of the Two Micron All Sky Survey (2MASS), a joint project of the University of Massachusetts and the Infrared Processing and Analysis Center/California Institute of Technology, funded by the National Aeronautics and Space Administration and the National Science Foundation.

Book Design, Editing, and Layout by Aaron Rose, Mount Shasta, California

Publications by Mary Saint-Marie:
 Galactic Shamanism
 The Holy Sight
 Messages from the Silence
 The Sacred Two
 The Star-Stone Ones
 The Animating Presence
 The Monitor and Laughter of the Gods
 Art As Consciousness
 The Oracle and the Dreamer

*This book is dedicated to Balance…
upon this little spinning orb we know as Earth…*

*And this book is dedicated to Consciousness…
that directs this Balance…*

Contents

Acknowledgments *11*
Preface *13*
Introduction *15*

Part One: Galactic Shamanism

World Birth *19*
The Star-Stone Ones *21*
Landing the Archetypal Realm Templates *27*

Part Two: Odysseys into Non-Time

SHE…it is…who Remembers *43*
A Journey from the Stars unto the Stones *61*
Galactic Shamanism *71*
Message from Spotted Owl *75*
The Earth is Already Saved *81*

Part Three: Awareness from the Invisible Realms

Galactic Shamanism Journeys 89
Journey through the Kingdoms and the Elements 89

Teachings from Higher Dimensions and Original Archetypes Realms 105

The Realm of Pure Energy: Be Here Now (1971) 111

The Soul Realm of Joy: Near-Death Experience (1971) 115

The Cosmic Birthing Force: Birthing Experience (1975) 119

Inner Music Realms: Angelic, Celestial, and Music of the Spheres (1978 and on) 123

Realm of Cosmic Consciousness: I Am Awareness (1981) 128

The Blue Kachina Realm: A Visitation from Realm of Purity (1987) 133

Changing Woman Realm: Visitations (1980s) 141

Spider Woman Realm: Visitation (late 1980s) 144

White Buffalo Calf Woman Realm: Visitation 147

The Beatific Realm (1980s and later) 150

EarthCare Global TV: A Vision and Impartation (1996 and 1997) 154

The Animal Soul Realm:
Visitations and Messages (1996 and on) 156

The Overlighting:
Visitation and Healing (on trip to Brazil) 159

The Realm of Illumination:
Perfection Manifest (2013) 163

The Leap off the Metaphoric Cliff (1971) 165

The Great Mother: An Embodiment (2016) 171

Part Four:
Afterwords

About the Title 179

About the Writing Style 179

About the Art 181

About the Sacred Two 181

About the Male Archetype 181

About Life as Living Ceremony 182

About the Changes:
Prophecies are Messengers of Change 186

About the Artist-Writer 189

Biography and Education 191

Art, CDs, Soul Sessions, and Soul Retreats 193

EarthCare Global TV 201

The Art

The Rainbow Dream…of Beauty-SHE 14

Star-Stone Essence-SHE 42

Golden-eyed Ancient Beauty-SHE…sings the song of songs…46

Journey-SHE…from the Stars unto the Stones… 60

Native-HE…dances with birds…....................................70

Starry Mantle of Spirit...74

and together…they dream and sing of worlds unseen……..80

Beauty-SHE and HE…Embraced by the Universe............88

Changing Woman Star Dance 104

Sky-Dancer SHE 114

Journey-HE…from the Stars unto the Stones 132

SHE…of the Circle..146

Greetings from the Stars 170

Acknowledgments

I deeply thank Walter and Law Russell and Joel Goldsmith for their guidance in attunement to the One.

There are many other teachers and teachings that continue to guide and I thank them all. I thank the ones in all dimensions who have inspired me to greater depths of my Being, to greater expression of my self, that I may give richly to others.

I wish to thank my loved daughters, Kimberly and Rebecca, both of whom have seen my multi-birthings of consciousness (some were difficult) and who both gave me the gift of motherhood…a most precious gift.

I thank my mother, one of the early pioneering American female pilots and Air Force instructors, who supported me in endless ways.

I am in great gratitude to all my friends. Your presence in my life makes it easier to retreat into solitude of creativity.

And I thank dear one, Solara, for coming in my dreams, telling me that it was time to write and publish.

I thank all of Nature for such a reflection for us all.

I thank my Soul group beyond the stars.

And I thank Aaron Rose, who has helped to ground this second edition. Working with one who is technically adept is such a gift. And working with one who can attune to the soul of the book is extraordinary. A joyful journey!

Preface

"Together…we are in the Soul's Remembering."

Shared in this book…
is a personal odyssey and its translation into the Impersonal,
when seen through the eye of the Soul,
where wisdom and love do marry and know.

Shared in this book…
is the experience of Soul as a state of Consciousness
rather than a subject of conjecture.

Shared in this book…
is entry into the Land of the Now,
the "once upon a non-time" of the ever talked about garden.
This planetary initiation into the One Soul is upon us all.

Shared in this book…
is the "Collective World Birth of Balance,"
as is happening NOW,
as the Archetypal Feminine arises
and takes its rightful place beside the Archetypal Masculine.
HE and SHE…
of the every present Yin-Yang Circle known of old.

"We no longer need to create the near-death experiences
of accidents and diseases, drugs or tragedy,
to have breakthrough experiences into the Light.

The Light of the Soul ever beckons from within."

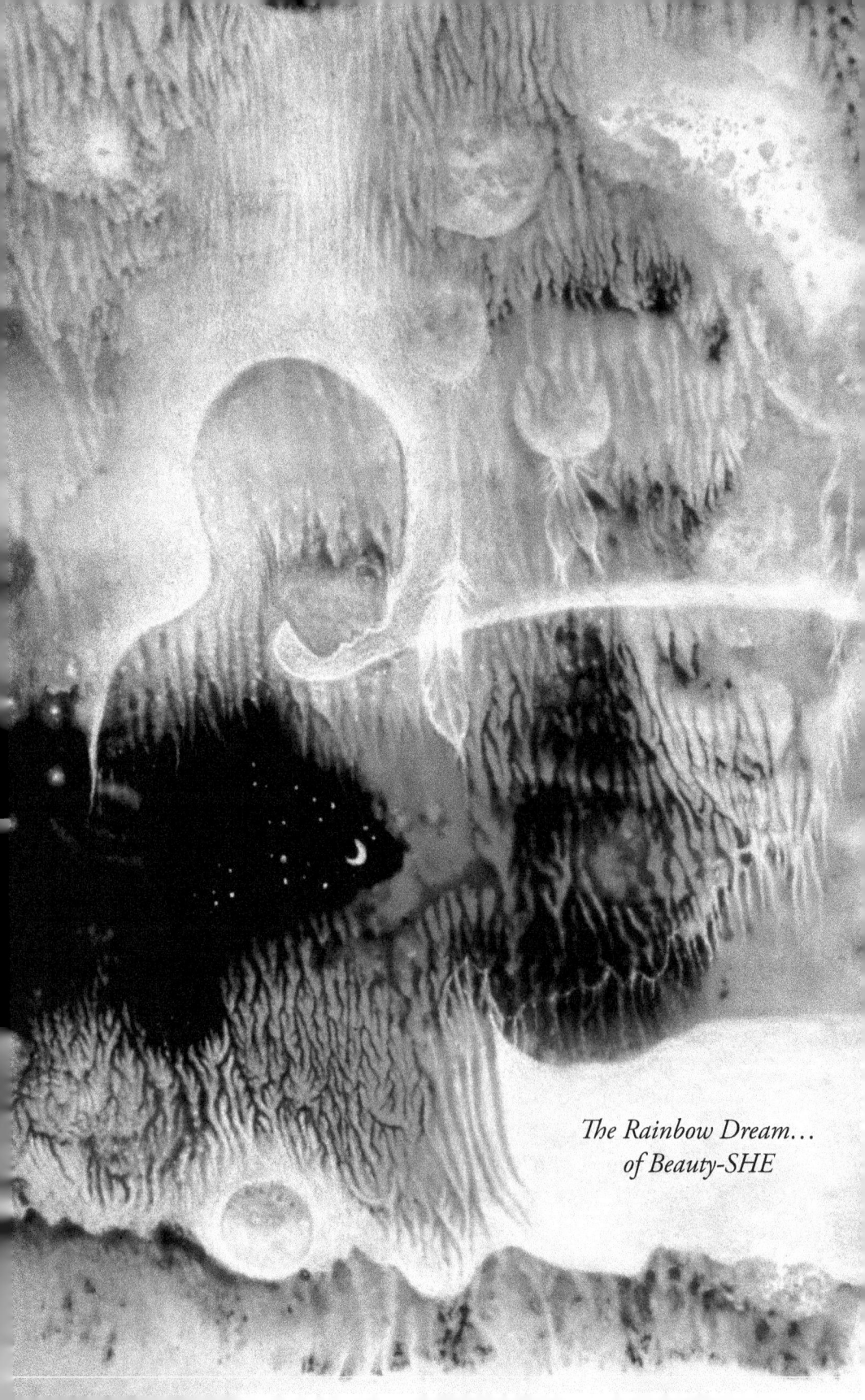

*The Rainbow Dream…
of Beauty-SHE*

Introduction

The Sacred Passage of Beauty-SHE

This book is about the unveilings of the archetypal feminine, in both man and in woman, that is happening unto this very time and unto this approaching non-time. When a man or a woman goes into the Silence, one must approach with the feminine, the receptive. One must approach empty, ready to be filled. One must approach as a vessel, a grail cup, a songless flute, or as the archetypal yoni. It is a sacred moment and it is a moment of Trust. Men and women everywhere must go to the Silence to receive the ONE. There is only ONE. Much of the global family is now opening to ONEness and is consciously accessing, exploring, and revealing the ancient mysteries. I offer these "Odysseys into Non-Time" to reflect, feel, inspire, and remember…the collective multi-cultural, multi-dimensional journey we are all on, that we may "land the inner vision unto these very times."

These words and sacred art are based on my inner journeys, visions, and experiences with the Presence of the ONE, of Universal Soul, since 1972. They came as I meditated on the Presence of God.

Together…we are making the Sacred Passage of Beauty-SHE, of Archetypal Woman. There, in the inner realms, SHE beholds Universal Visions. There, in the inner realms, SHE remembers HER-Dance upon the Earth. And there it is that the birth begins. And then will begin, by man and woman, the HE and SHE of Creation, ceremonial enactments of Spirit. Then will begin Sacred Enactments of Ancient Remembering.

And comes…multi-cultural blendings and bleed-throughs of all cultures and of all times, merged with the multi-dimensional, the galactic, the "once upon a non-time"…the long awaited enactments of Galactic Shamanism.

We are unto those very times.

Part One:

Galactic Shamanism

World Birth

There is happening on this planet at this time an unprecedented World Birth. It is a World Birth of the Universal Soul. The ONE. For each to be a conscious part of this World Birth they must leave the prodigal journey of seeming separation and return to the ONE. To return to the ONE, the Beloved within, each must become receptive and go into the Silence. To become receptive, both men and women must access their feminine nature. Each must deeply open and become empty, as the grail cup waiting to be filled with nectar of Spirit.

This en masse knowing to come into the feminine is causing very great changes on the planet in men and in women. It is not only woman coming into the Priestess, the Goddess, the Archetypal, ONE-woman Consciousness, but men are also feeling and finding their receptive feminine nature, both within and without. What we are experiencing is the collective rising of the feminine principle in man and in woman. It is rising globally to enact the balanced and equal partner with the masculine energies already on the planet. When each has returned to the ONE, they will have found their own inner masculine and feminine. Then they can dance their own polarity, both within and without. They will walk in Balance.

The World Birth of Universal Soul now happening brings in its wake the living of World Balance. This new and conscious awareness of Balance by man and by woman will birth new forms. These new forms will be enacted in many ways. They are The Sacred Enactments of Ancient Remembering. As these enactments occur, we shall witness the union of opposites, the marriage of earth and sky, of day and night. We shall see "the Angels that land and the Shamans that fly." We shall be in the world and not of the world. This is "the landing of the Divine Archetypal Realms."

This is Galactic Shamanism. The marriage of the above and the below. There is only ONE. The ONE Dance already is, if we will but tune in and enact our part. And we must honor also the enacting of all other parts. The ancient "namaste"—which means to honor the Divine in another, no matter what the appearance—must be lived. The lack of honor to Self and other Selves has kept us all in a sense of seeming separation. No more.

We are in the times of The Sacred Enactments of Ancient Remembering. We are all learning to allow "the landing of the Archetypal Realms." We are finding a "landing pad," that we may live the ONE Dream. This happens only when we find the Beloved within. It is the inner ONE that is the balance of the masculine and feminine dance in each of us. It is then that we know the state of mind that is Galactic Shamanism. It is Balance. It is Grace. Together we enter the collective World Birth of Universal Soul, the World Birth of Balance, the World Birth of Grace.

In this World Birth, we witness unprecedented Living Ceremonies of the Soul. In this World Birth, we see unprecedented numbers of balanced men and women. They now arrive Two by Two. They are The Sacred Twos, HE and SHE. The Archetypal Realm of Divine Consciousness is ever waiting to be accessed and landed upon this little spinning orb we know as Earth. It is ready to be enacted. Together…let us…enact the Eternal!

The Star-Stone Ones

Each one of us shall know Galactic Shamanism. It is when our eyes are on the stars and our feet are on the ground. It is the being in the world, but not of the world. It is beyond the conceptual realm. It is an experience beyond human words, human thoughts, and human time. It is of the wordless and the nameless. It is beyond naming. Even the words Galactic Shamanism are only used to trigger and catalyze…to inspire Remembering. Then, they too shall fall away.

Galactic Shamanism is a state of consciousness. It is a state of consciousness that we can live. It is a state of Balance. It is like touching the Impersonal and allowing it to have a Life. Your Life. It is a touching of a place I call Star-Stone Essence, deep within the Soul, the One Universal Soul. To be Galactic, we open our consciousness out to the stars, the sky, and expanded out to the ever present Isness. We remember our starry origins. We remember the music of the spheres. We remember the angelic realms. We remember the archetypal realms. We remember the "many mansions." We remember consciousness in invisible realms. To be Shamanic, we open our consciousness to the primal, the indigenous, the stone and earth of our nature. We can hear the very rocks; we feel the omnipresence of Spirit flow through all Nature; we merge in consciousness with the visible world, with Creation.

We come into Galactic Shamanism simply, very simply…by going to the ONE. Our starry essence and our stone essence merge and we experience ourselves as Star-Stone Ones. We experience Star-Stone Essence. We experience Balance.

In 1971, I had my second opening to Inner Vision of the

Universal Soul, the ONEness. I was driving my car to work early one morning. I was driving the long way, along a beautiful back road through Nature. There was a light snow falling. A car coming in the opposite direction went out of control just as we neared one another. It was too late to swerve or brake on the slippery road, so we had a head-on collision. The last words I thought were, "I'm yours, God." At the moment of impact, I saw my life—past, present and future—via my Soul. I did not even comprehend Soul before the crash. There was pure ecstasy and understanding. I knew in that instant that my life was perfect. After the impact, I lost the memory of the details that came before me in that instant, but I remembered the Soul Essence, the sweetness of Spirit.

After the crash which my totaled car, in which I was not even scratched, I could see the white light glowing from around people, plants, and animals…really, all living things. My vision could now see the glowing essence of the light body. Some people call that altered vision. I would say human consciousness has altered vision. I had opened into the beginnings of true vision, sight into the invisible realms. Time would pass before my inner vision opened, even much more, to reveal unto me even my starry origins, who I am, and why I am here.

After the collision, I became more discontented daily with my safe, secure, and stable position as English and Communications instructor at a community college. In the impact of the collision, I had seen my true Life through a literary template, so to speak. I had seen my Life via my Soul through the actual structure of James Joyce's book, *Finnegan's Wake*. It was a book I never could fathom. That was probably the only avenue Spirit could reach my then trained academic mind…at the time. It worked. I was now very discontented and intuitively knew there was much more to learn, to explore, to experience. I could not remember with my conscious mind what it was. It did not matter. I finally had a glimpse of "the Kingdom is Within."

I quit the teaching position, and with a few art supplies, one change of clothing, a sleeping bag, and Kelty pack, left for cultures that called to me. I needed to experience the heart and soul and beauty of cultures not stuck in left-brain technology. I spent nearly six months in Africa, Spain, Crete, Greece, Turkey, Afghanistan, Iran, Pakistan, India, and Kashmir.

Slowly, very slowly, the consciousness of Galactic Shamanism began to dawn. I wish to note that I was doing no spiritual practices when I was spontaneously "bumped" into the higher realms in the car collision. Nor was I eating any of the multitude of diets. I was just beginning to read about spirituality. The experience came through Grace. Rememberings are happening all around us…through Grace.

I began to meditate on the ONE. That continued to open my consciousness. The inner experiences were many, and as I began to leave imbalanced man-woman relationships behind, I began to hear the Music of the Spheres when I would go into the inner silence.

Finally in 1981, I understood Galactic Shamanism in a more expansive way. For nine hours in meditation (from nine o'clock one evening until six the next morning) I sat at the "edge of paradox." At the "crack of the universe." I witnessed that all was both in me and outside of me simultaneously. And the me that witnessed this was both the Presence and Mary…the Impersonal and the personal…also simultaneously. I was pure consciousness, the Presence, watching it all. I realized each of us can access the place where we do Know. In that Knowing, there is no one outside our Self to call to. No guides, no angels, no masters, no preachers, no mediums, no readers, no channels, no geometries. There is only ONE. In that ONEness, we Know. It is simply Consciousness. Pure Awareness.

This experience of Galactic Shamanism is when the invisible and the visible are ONE. The form and the formless are ONE. It changes one's life forever. For then, there is no desire to separate and call forth something outside ourselves. The Kingdom is Within. We need only merge with the ONE. Revelations come.

Although I must now learn to maintain and sustain that state of consciousness, there was enough revealed to live my life anew. From the place of Galactic Shamanism, there is only a desire to allow that consciousness to come through and express and create in movement, sound, or form. In the ONEness, we become the Revelations. We are the Living Revelations. And in the Living Revelations…do we become the Life as Living Ceremony.

In 1984, I awoke in the middle of the night and, in an instant, I experienced and saw the galaxies, stars, universes through my physical body. I was given to know our body form as the Temple Template of Infinity. Sacred. When the experiences come, they do not seem to me like what the world calls peak experiences or even mystical experiences. In that moment they are Reality and what the world calls reality is but a finite seeming. They are natural. They are more of who we all really are. They are of the wordless and the nameless.

So all these many years I continued to share of what I experienced of Universal Soul through paintings and sculpture. Sacred Art allowed me an opening through which to share that which I did know, even if they were but glimpses into Infinity. Though I saw, in an instant, the human body as the Temple Template of Infinity, it took many years of preparation to give it outer expression.

The veils are falling and each shall find ways to express the mysteries. Then it is that individuals shall gather more and more with like-minded ones to share Galactic Shamanism in groups and communities. And, most especially, they shall begin to come together as The Sacred Two, the balanced men and women who come together as the united ONE.

In 1987, I finally began to hear within, the actual words Galactic Shamanism, over and over, and starting in June of that year, my experiences both in meditation and living ceremony began to increase. The ceremonies that Spirit created spontaneously through me were the grounding of the invisible into the visible. It was what I call Star-Stone mergings. I was awakening as a Star-Stone One. It is what Black Elk referred to when he spoke of living one's vision, or sickness comes. Give a body to your vision. Give a form to your vision. Ground your Vision. Land your galactic vision in a shamanic way. Create a landing pad! Take the ascension of consciousness and live it on the 3-D. To do that we must become birthers of new ceremonial spaces to share the new forms. We can do whatever it takes to share our part in the global dance of Galactic Shamanism, the Dance of the Star-Stone Ones.

From this consciousness of ONEness, new forms may flow from within. They are our "Odysseys into Non-Time." There we can Remember, hear, see, know, BE! All of the "Odysseys into Non-Time" shared in this book began their pouring forth from Consciousness, beginning at pre-dawn, dawn, and finally into the new day. Each day…a new day…a new consciousness can dawn. Never to be repeated, reproduced, or lived again. Always, in my writing, the words were just there, directed from the ONE.

Imagine the changes of Western culture, that has so often grown bored with its 9 to 5, Monday to Friday, sterile patterns of technology. To find an outlet into non-time, it has often greatly turned to alcohol, sex, and drugs. It is a temporary seduction, caused by imbalance, that will only be remedied in "non-time," in the Silence, in the ONEness.

And finally came the revelation that at the beginning of the nineties tradition began to rapidly dissolve. The sweet and powerful traditions, that we have all indeed needed, in our lives of seeming separation from the ONE, for they kept the Light alive in a dark world. In the section of Life as Living Ceremony, I share more of the revelation which came to me of traditions dissolving. I share about the changes that are allowed as we move into the receptive SHE of our nature, first individually and then collectively. Then…it is…that we can know and experience that which the SHE of all creation does bring to all unto these very times. And the Star-Stone Ones do come…

Landing the Archetypal Realm Templates

awa tey ewa tey
Now is the Time
to land the inner vision
of the Archetypal Realm

In the following odysseys into non-time, I have revealed some of my personal journeys and experiences into the Impersonal, Archetypal Realms of the Divine, not so much to tell my story, as to reveal that there is, in truth, only One Story and we are all players upon the stage. An Archetypal experience touches all. It uplifts all.

I am sharing about the Landing of the Archetypal Realms upon this physical plane of existence. I am sharing about the Archetypal Tale…from the Land of the Now. I am sharing to remind us that first we must have inner vision and inner knowing and then we must anchor it, land it, ground it, by enacting it in some way. We must give the Love that is this vision…a body, a form.

This can be done in so many ways. Infinite ways. But it is imperative to act it out. We came to act it out. To land it. It is how we fulfill our dream, in the ONE Dream. We must pass through the doors from the fear realms. From there we become the galactic knowing, acting on the Earth as a shaman. And again Galactic Shamanism. The Living Ceremony of Spirit is Galactic Shamanism. As above, so below.

We can land the vision in many ways. We can simply create an object to share with others. An object to be filled with essence. A grail filled with the Soul's nectar. It is our gift. It may be an invention, a painting, a song, a meal, a house, a cup of tea. We can grow a flower or an apple tree. We can knit a sweater or make a drum. We can write a play or write a poem. It all is Ceremony, Ceremony of the Eternal.

Or we can share the intangible. A story, a prayer or simply a smile. Tangible or intangible. Visible or invisible. No matter. It is to be expressed and shared. Give the formless essence form. Again…it is all Ceremony, Living Ceremony of the Soul.

That is Love. That is Love expressed. That is Living Ceremony of Spirit. That is Galactic Shamanism. That is the Holy Marriage.

Are you ready to receive your vision? Are you ready to be with God? Are you ready to land your vision? Are you ready to live in a world free of intercessors and intermediaries? Free of ones between you and God? Free of objects between you and God?

Outer guides and teachers and tools are wonderful ways of preparing the soil of the mind, making it fertile, by adding something from without so that it is made ready to receive Spirit, Divine Mind, the Consciousness of the ONE. When human mind and God Mind begin to merge, unite as ONE, the need for intercessors begins to fall away.

Intercessors are valuable, also, to bring Remembrance of the One Power and to inspire. A ritual, for example, acts as a sacred container for Truth. And finally, when our very Being is ready to be the container, the holy vessel for the inner splendor…the Truth…the outer container can fall away. Be ever ready.

Following is my personal story of how and when it became time in my life to share what I had seen in "non-time," to share what I had seen of the Archetypal Templates to be landed unto these very times. I call the story "awa tey ewa tey."

It was 1989 and I was walking in the meadows, near the forest by my Mount Shasta home. Day after day, on my solitary walks in the silence of Nature, I would hear from the inner realms, "awa tey ewa tey." Repeatedly I would ask inwardly, "What does that mean?"

I loved the sounds. They would echo in my mind. One day as I walked and as I prayed deeply to know, I heard, "Now is the Time."

Simultaneously came a phone call from a friend who told me she felt deeply to share a book with me. It was *Black Elk Speaks*. I was not in a reading mode and had great resistance, but with her persuasion, I decided to begin. I read fast, looking for the message that was there for me, and toward the end of the book I found it. There it was…the call to look at the "time." The same message again.

It became clear to me that "Now is the Time" meant that Now is the Time for the World Birth. It was also the time for me to be who I am fully, to live my vision, my own seemingly personal enactment of Spirit as had been revealed. Individual birth brings collective world birth. Together…we are the World Birth…

Our seemingly personal journeys in combination with others are a grand paradox. It is both personal and Impersonal. It is literally the combinations, the chemical formulas, the alchemical unions that will birth the greater, expanded, more enlightened Consciousness. It is the One Story, the Sacred Enactment of Ancient Remembering. It is Galactic Shamanism.

Our sacred acts, birthed from within, from our seemingly personal truth, are the sacred geometries, the soul glyphs, the literal keys and configurations that open and ground and land the cosmic vision, the ONE vision into the ONE Dance. It is the Dance of the One as the Many.

awa tey ewa tey
Now is the Time…
to land the visions…

Since 1972, I have translated the energies of inner vision into Sacred and Universal Art of the Soul and Ceremony of the Soul. By sharing these experiences now in words, it is my prayer that I may inspire others to land their inner vision from the ONE vision. The World Birth can only happen by everyone birthing their inner vision, their own true knowing. To do that, they must be connected inwardly. And to do that, they must go direct to the ONE.

Now is the Time…

En masse we must find the paradox, that is, the personal vision, that is really the Impersonal vision, the ONE vision. We must allow it to be lived through us and as us.

Then…it is…
that we shall re-give what we are given from within…

Then…it is…
that we shall re-inspire others with our enactment…

Then…it is…
that original inspiration from Creator shall grace the lands…

Not only has Black Elk released this message of living one's vision, but also William Blake, the English poet and artist, who knew that those with no vision shall perish. And again it is revealed in Proverbs. Vision is our map.

This book is about "landing" sacred visions, divine inspirations and cosmic revelations. This "landing" is the Living Ceremony of Spirit. It is Life. These visions are there for all of us if we will make ourselves ready and prepare the soil of our minds to receive, that our very being may be a template to express and be the outpouring of the splendor of Spirit.

Collectively we are preparing to "land the Divine" consciously. We must prepare the body to land it. And we must prepare our "landing pad," our space in the Garden of Earth, to enact our part in the play.

It is an unspeakable enactment, unfathomable by the human mind. This preparation will make us aware of every moment in the Now. When we are aware, each moment is alive, light filled, giving us the cosmic story.

We are the very revelations. When our consciousness is aligned with the Divine, we literally enact the cosmic story. We are the cosmic stars…come unto the stones. We are the Star-Stone Ones who gather as The Star-Stone Twos, enacting the Star-Stone Ceremonies of the Star-Stone Tribes. We are the very Journey of the Stars unto the Stones. The Soul Tribes…they do gather…

We are the cosmic mergings. It is beyond any Hollywood script. You will see yourself and everyone and everything as a "star," a sparkling light on this plane of affairs. When seen in this sparkling light, life cannot be dual, monotonous or boring, nor can it be tedious or a struggle. It is simply Soul expressing. It is utterly so simple as to be missed by the illusion of mental complexity, especially that known to us in the Western culture.

Our culture has gained great skills with mental prowess, which has given us many comforts, efficiencies and instant global communication. But without the Essence borne of Spirit, the mental is as a lost child, always spreading and breeding pain and fear. We must be receptive now to the "inner vision." It is Time. And then comes…World Birth!

>Then…it is…
>that we know ourselves
>as translators…interpreters of Spirit…
>
>Then…it is…
>that we know ourselves
>as expressions of Spirit…
>
>Then…it is…
>that Creation can unfold…
>according to the Plan…consciously…
>
>Then…it is…
>that Joy can reign…and
>
>Then…it is…
>that we can realize…
>we are the revelation…
>we are Source revealed…
>we are Light manifest…

So search as one will in the outer orbs or in the ever human mind, one will never find that for which one searches.

Search…ye need not…
Only open…open to Divine Consciousness…
Direct…with no intercessors or intermediaries
on the physical or non-physical realms…
Be open and receptive…only to the ONE…

It is Time
Now is the Time
awa tey ewa tey

And Now is the Time for me to reveal the holy splendor of one of my cosmic glimpses, known by the ancients as the rapture. Since 1972, I have rarely shared my illuminations, my glimpses. I have been silent, except to a few, when I was guided to share and I knew the information to be a catalyst. It is my prayer that this sharing eliminates years of outer searching for ones in quest of a spiritual life, in full expression of their true identity.

May this sharing serve as an inspiration in other lives.

The glimpse happened in 1981 and lasted for nine hours, from nine one evening until six the next morning. I was beyond comprehension of the ever human mind. Although mystical experiences began spontaneously in 1972, this one was the opening when I realized "Source" was our teacher.

In this glimpse, I came to know what I call "sitting at the edge of paradox," between form and formless. I saw the wisdom of living in and not of the world. I saw who I am. I saw, too, that All are. For there is only One. I want to clearly state that I was not channeling or going into astral realms. It was a clear, lucid awareness of Being. I was aware of Self as pure Consciousness. I Am Awareness.

Here is how it happened. I was meditating with another. I sat down to contemplate and meditate on the One. The soil of my mind was fertile, ready and receptive to accept expanded, deepened inner knowing. First, I heard a dog bark outside. Simultaneously I experienced and actually realized the dog as creation in my consciousness. It was within and without all at once. Then I heard a car go by. I had the same awareness.

I just continued to open to what was unfolding in inner consciousness. I said Yes! Then I had the experience with my home. Then I saw all of the Mount Shasta village both within and without. I continued to open and expand. Then I saw all of the West Coast, both within and without. And still I opened. Finally I saw our entire country within me and without. I continued to open and expand. Next I saw all of Planet Earth both in me and out of me. I continued to open, to say yes wordlessly and expand consciousness.

Until now, it was as if these things were all both within and without my body and my consciousness. As I continued to expand into the star systems, there was an etheric remnant of my physical form, where I could perceive and know directly the cosmos as both within and without, both my consciousness and the etheric remnant. It is difficult to share as expression in words.

Finally there was only Consciousness, the Presence. I was aware that I Am. For a while, this pure awareness "traveled" throughout the star systems and galaxies. The entire experience was pure ecstasy, beyond human joy. Emotions as humans perceive them do not exist in this state of consciousness. There is only an ecstatic state of knowing.

When I "returned," so to speak, I realized that my personal path was direct with Spirit, not thorough intercessors of times past.

I realized that true teachers and educators would teach others how to go direct to God. They, being free, would help to set others free, through the examples of their lives and teachings.

I very soon had to learn two things. One was that sharing my experience with ones who were not open or did not ask was not wise. I was not to exercise arrogance and try to free them from their chosen path. I was not to judge or change their path. Just Namaste.

I also had to learn that cosmic glimpses are not full illuminations. They are just that…glimpses. And even the tiniest glimpse into the Realm of the Real can fully change the course of one's life. The most difficult part of "returning to time and space as we know it" was honoring how much time I needed personally to integrate the reality I had glimpsed, before I could even begin to consider application and practice, thus live it. Once this reality has been visited, one is ever discontent with life as it was.

I have not been inspired to write about this experience since 1981. I was only inspired to paint and sculpt the Beauty of the Soul and to create Ceremony with Sounds and Signings of the Soul. In this way, I could remember. I could remember who I really was. And the experiences continued. I was "drawing and painting" out of my very own Being, the grand Remembering. My inner vision continued to open and the glimpses continued to come, asking always "to be landed unto these very times."

When I went within, I always went only to the One, to God, to Spirit. And Spirit journeyed me. The glimpses continued.

Sometime in 1984, I awoke in the night and spontaneously went into the consciousness where I saw all of the cosmos throughout my physical body, which I learned to call the "Temple Template of Infinity." I saw that humans can know Self as the One Presence.

As the years continued, so did my commitment to merge my outer reality with what I had had revealed on the inner. I had to be patient with myself and honor and respect all the time it seemed to be taking to integrate the information and be able to live in the presence and trust the Presence. The outer unfolding of the inner vision journey continued.

I learned next to quit debating reality and concepts with others. I no longer needed to get them to see what I had seen. I learned compassion and I learned to honor their chosen Path to the One. The most difficult thing for me to let go of was sympathy. I would merge inappropriately with the "poor me" dramas of others, calling it friendship. It was a very slow unfoldment for a time, but I made the shift and learned to grow in the living from within.

All this time I continued to learn from the One. I did not actually just see a vision, but I was right there in the Realm of the Real where Creation can be known, before it lands on the physical plane. All is ecstatic in these realms. I continued to paint and sculpt the experiences. Time unfolded out of non-time. Instead of merging inappropriately with painful or fearful situations, I learned to trust the revelations from the Realms of the Real, waiting to be landed unto these very times.

awa tey ewa tey
Now is the Time

I share in this book my personal experiences of the Impersonal.

I share to inspire remembering. I share to inspire about remembering though inner vision and inner knowing and inner listening. And I share to inspire the Sacred Enactments of Ancient Remembering to be landed by the collective. Together… let us odyssey into the "once upon a non-time" of inner realms and enact this World Birth.

What I have beheld on the inner planes are Divine Archetypes. They are not psychological concepts to be ever studied, analyzed and researched. They are a realm of reality. They can be experienced. One merges with the experience, assimilates it and finally expresses it. These archetypes are keepers of divine qualities to be lived upon the physical plane.

Finally, I realized that my own personal issue in the "landing" of what I could see and know on the inner planes was trust. Trust in the Divine. Trust is the link that allows one to manifest the inner knowing outwardly. Otherwise, one remains a dreamer. One teaches the galactic but not the shamanic. One has a dream, but no fulfillment.

With trust, we have the alabaster marriage, the divine union of earth and sky, the above and below. The opposites dissolve and there is only One. Galactic Shamanism. No separation. That is the Balance.

Part Two:
Odysseys into Non-Time

The following Odysseys into Non-Time come from my experiences of sitting at the edge of paradox, where the visible and invisible merge. It is the place in the Void where I access Sacred and Mystical Art…the images of Universal Soul. I did not decide to finally give words, instead of images, to these experiences. The words kept coming. The revelations kept coming. I had actually considered burning all my journals, for even for me, some of it was Way out there.

Here is a long story cut short. I became extremely sick from an art product, sold my home, and moved to the desert in the Southwest, to live in an adobe art studio and quietly paint and sculpt my revelations. It has not turned out such. I was moved instead to the high desert, about fifteen miles from my previous mountain home, into a twelve-sided dome home, a further fulfillment of the ceremonial circle I have felt for years. Once there, I again picked up my pen to share my experiences.

Now begin the Odysseys into Non-Time.

Star-Stone Essence-SHE

O' Maiden of the Stars…
Come ye unto the stones…
and be at Home
Far have ye traveled…
and there is yet a ways to go…

SHE...it is...who Remembers

Woman: The Dancer of Love's Dance...

All contained in this odyssey...are examples...given from individual experience...

This odyssey is offered as a gift... to reinspire others to journey inward and find their own Knowing...their own expression...their own symbols...

It is offered to reinspire others to quit relying on mates, family, friends, psychics and counselors to access your knowing for you. It is true that at times we truly can use help...but make sure that help...is helping you become connected to Source, connected to the One...

Avoid ones who continue to access for you, thus leaving you disempowered and needing them a next time. If you truly need help, find someone who can guide you on your inward journey to Self...

These experiences and journeys into the inner Realms of the Real, the "once upon a non-time," dream time, have each given me a teaching. Teachings from the Archetypal Realms.

Each teaching...must be lived on this plane of existence...and through the living of the message of the Teachings from the Realms, one can begin to share of the teaching, of the message, of the Remembering...of the experience of Ecstasy...awaiting us each moment we are present...in the Presence of the One...

Note to man and to woman:

Archetypal Woman in this book becomes an outer symbol for the feminine principle, the receptive in man and in woman.

And this feminine is the initiator of fusion upon this globe. We must together create a world that once again allows all the True inner gifts of the feminine to be expressed.

Introduction

This story is a poetic and visual Odyssey of one woman's Remembering...

HER-Remembering
of who SHE is and why SHE is here...

HER-Remembering
of her Journey of the Stars unto the Stones...

HER-Remembering
of her Star-Stone Essence...

HER-Remembering
of her planet beyond the stars...
and her dance upon the earth...

HER-Remembering
of the wordless and the nameless...
traveling and journeying to realms and dimensions
where desire never rises...to name or time...

HER-Remembering
that knowing is spherical...

HER-Remembering
of the Sacred Archetypal woman dance
in other realms and dimensions...
to be landed...unto these times...

HER-Remembering
that these are archetypal realms...
and that they are true for all
though each would translate or interpret
through their own unique expression...

And you might ask...how did these Rememberings come... Simply...very simply...by going to the ONE. Each must find one's own path for going to the ONE.

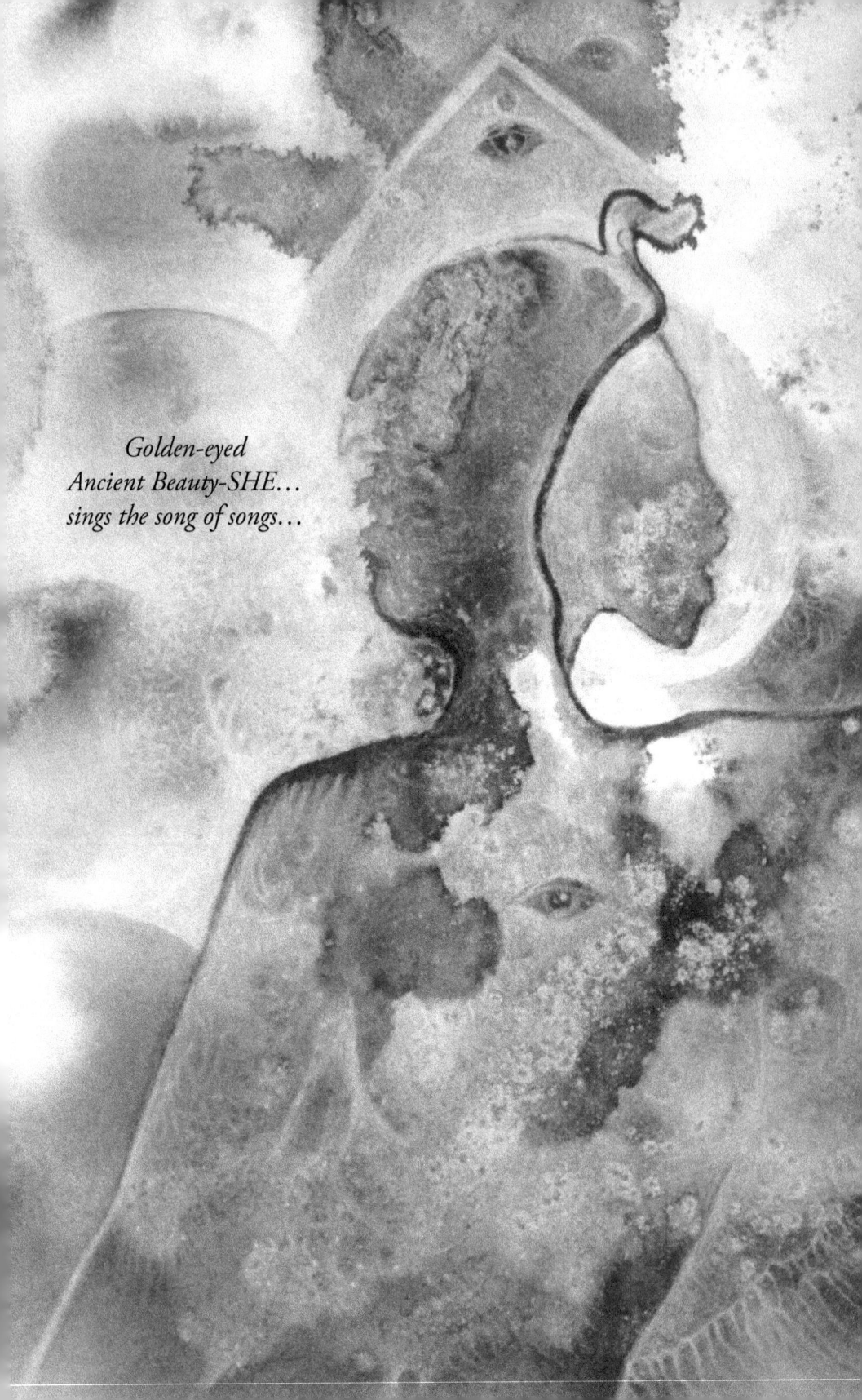

SHE...it is...who Remembers

Woman! Who is Woman?
Woman is the *Dancer of Love's Dance*
and the *Singer of Love's Song*.

Woman throughout history, which is time, has been suppressed from being Her true Self.

Now is the Time...for woman to step forward and do her dance... to step forward and sing the *Song of Songs*...

Woman-SHE...it is...
Beauty-SHE...of all the fairy tales...
who needs to do the Dance.

Woman-SHE...it is...who needs to tell her-story.

It is not a story of competition with man.
It is not a story of the man race.
It is not a story of the battle of the sexes.
It is not a story of making it in the business world.
It is not a story of glamour,
nor a story of marketing on Wall Street.

I say unto you...It is the story of Love.
It is a story of Love's Dance and Love's Body...

Woman in her natural estate is LOVE.

As Conscious LOVE...
SHE...it is...who travels and journeys into the Realms...
SHE...it is...who journeys into the dimensions...
SHE...it is...who journeys past the stars...
SHE...it is...who journeys beyond the beyond...
and SHE...it is...who reveals the land of the dimensionless...

Yes…Beauty-SHE…of all the fairy tales…
can journey into the sky…
And Beauty-SHE…of all the fairy tales…
can journey into the earth…

SHE…it is…
who can journey into the earth
and see the very glowing of the Christed rocks…

SHE…it is…
who can journey into the archetypal animal kingdom…
and see their very souls…
and see their ceremonies…
and hear their wordless message:
"we await the human kingdom…
we will ceremony with and for you…we await…"

SHE…it is…
who sees the animal kingdom…
already Christed…glowing in pristine Love…

SHE…it is…
who journeys into archetypal realms
and sees the Woman Dance…

SHE…it is…
who Remembers…

SHE…it is…
who dares…to Remember…
to Remember the way it Really is…

Remembering…
Woman…is Remembering…
It is the time for Woman to Remember…

It is time for her to Remember the female archetypes…
It is time for her to Remember who she is…

SHE…is Changing Woman…
the ever changing formless form…
that moves easily from form to formless,
from earth to sky…
that knows the marriage of day and night…
that becomes the very stars…
and blows as the very wind…

SHE…Changing Woman…
is the one who merges…

SHE can merge with the sound of a waterfall…
SHE can merge with the hardest stones
until they reveal their very sound…
and the primordial's tone is known…

O Ye Woman…
the enchantress, the dreamer of dreams…
Ye are the very Star-Stone Essence of Eternity.
Ye are the very Consciousness of Creation's Dance.
Ye are the Sacred Dance.

SHE…is Spider Woman…
the ONE who remembers…
that all women are ONE Woman…
the ONE who remembers…
that all women are doing the dance of Spider Woman…
the ONE Woman…
the ONE…who remembers
that woman…true woman has no jealousy, no envy,
no competitiveness, no lust…

SHE…it is…who remembers…
that Spider Woman embraces
the individual dance of Every Woman…
and each one adds to the *single archetypal dance
of Spider Woman…who fills the sky…*
And SHE…it is…who remembers the ecstasy of The Dance…
SHE…it is…who feels…the essence of The Dance…
And SHE…it is…who sees and Knows
woman's seashore dance…
as she dissolves…
becoming in a moment the sea, a wave, the sand,
and the blowing plants that Be…
And SHE…it is…who sees…
the glory and majesty of Archetypal Man…
watching…
watching the Archetypal Woman Dance…

HE…it is…who watches…
For HE…it is…who is triggered by Woman-SHE…
of all the fairy tales…

And SHE…is sky dancer…

SHE…it is…who remembers…Lemurian mergings…
SHE…it is…who remembers dissolving into the stars…
SHE…it is…who remembers the far and distant orbs…
SHE…it is…who remembers glimpses of who she is…

SHE remembers…
SHE remembers the body as *the Temple Template of Infinity…*
SHE sees the star systems throughout her body…
SHE Remembers…SHE is…Creation's Story…
SHE…is Universal-SHE…
SHE Remembers that *within* her consciousness
are the barking dogs,

the home she dwells in, the town, the state,
this little spinning orb she knows as Earth,
and on out into the galaxies.

SHE…it is…who knows and remembers…
essence that SHE is…
SHE…it is…who is *Creation's Dance*…
and SHE Remembers…

SHE Remembers outside the gates of time and space…
SHE Remembers outside dimension's doors…
SHE Remembers…Star-Stone Essence…
SHE Remembers…her flight…her *Journey*…
from the Stars unto the Stones…
SHE Remembers…SHE is Creation…

And SHE…is lifted…as it were…
unto *the Realm of the Blue Kachinas*
and Remembers the mystery of Woman
glowing with Love's Grace…in a circle of ten…

And SHE…it is…who enters the archetypal mouth…
a great cavern of darkness, in trust and perseverance…
There…it is…that she remembers the gods and goddesses,
the heroes and heroines of mythology's lore…
and ancient times of grandeur's NOW…

And SHE…remembers Beauty…
The Beauty of the *Dance of the Sacred Twos*…
The Beauty of the ONE…as the Sacred Two…
SHE…remembers the splendor of majestic Beauty…

And SHE…it is…who remembers…
the tribal chiefs of Ancient
appearing before archetypal-SHE…in inner realms…

one at a time appearing,
bowing before archetypal woman...

They are the ones who wait and know...
They are the great respecters of woman...
They are the holders of the vision...
They are the great Beholders of Beauty...

And SHE...it is...who remembers
the *realm of White Buffalo Woman*...
and the Dance of the Sacred Two...
within the circle of Infinity's Love...
the Yin-Yang circle known of ancient times...

And SHE...remembers...
who SHE is and from where she comes...
a planet beyond the stars...
and that which she does bring...

SHE...remembers...
dancing in the temples...
of Time's past
and in the other realms...
Then...ever slowly comes the movement
into the Present...into the Presence...
in Remembering NOW's Dance...

Woman...the ONE Woman...
Original...Archetypal Woman...
You are being beckoned...
You are being called...
Come forth...remember...
Reveal your dance...
Expose your Self...
Woman...drop thy veils...

We are the very mystery...
Unveil your mystery...
Remember...
And then begins...a new journey...
A journey of Creation's space
to do your dance...

Each woman is different, unique...
Each woman who returns to archetypal woman
and remembers...
adds to the collective thought of woman gathering
unto these very times...
That time is NOW...

Woman longs to be free of the talons of time!
SHE...it is...who is the *birther of new forms...*
SHE...it is...who births the formless into form...
SHE...it is...who feels the ecstasies
between the form and formless, visible and invisible...
SHE...it is...who remembers ecstasy...
The ecstasy of Being...
The ecstasy of Being Love...with no thought...
SHE...it is...who Remembers...

Come O ye woman...
Remember...
Add your remembering to the collective heart and mind...
Remember...there is but ONE Soul...
What you remember...adds to the All...

How do you Remember...
merge...o ye woman...
merge...with Infinity...
You...who as Changing Woman...know naturally
how to change from form to formless and back again...
who can merge with all that delights and enchants you...

Woman...
Merge...with all that is...
Dissolve...with all that is...
Become the very stars and the very earth...
Become the rarest flower on the mountain's edge...
Be the Light in the distant sky...
And then would ye ask...
And what shall I do with all this wondrous remembering...

Enact! Become the Living Enactment!
Create! Birth!
Birth new forms from your rememberings!
Find new ways to share your dance...
Give the Love...the Essence that you feel...
a form...a body...

Then...it is...that the new cosmology will begin
the birthings of a New Day...
Then...it is...that the princes and princesses
of all the fairy tales...can meet...
Then...it is...that we shall hear the fairy tales...
Then...it is...that we shall hear the stories
of "and they lived happily ever after...
and the story begins"...
the stories never told...for they were rarely lived...
Then...it is...that the stories will be told...

For archetypal woman...is true...original woman...
and she will draw nigh unto her...archetypal man...
and *together they will dance a new dance
unto Creation's Story...*
Her-Story will finally be added to His-Story
to make the True Story...the TruStory...
and the new world will begin...

These archetypal two hold the power
of the arc of the holy covenant…
They hold the vision of the new cosmology…
the ecstasy of the new world…

Their embrace in the Sacred Circle is Infinity's Sound…

This is not an ideal to be ever held in the human mind…
It is the opportunity to remember that…
NOW is the Time…
for woman to be truly free to express LOVE…
outside of social and cultural beliefs…
free to express True Woman…from the inside out…
free to reveal her dance…
free to be whole…

Woman…it is…who carries the *Gift of Ceremony*…
Not the sterile barrenness of repeated sameness…
as a stagnant ritual…
Rather the Living Ceremony…the Ceremony of Life…
the Ceremony of the NOW…

Woman…merge with the *Land of Now*…
and share your dance…

For woman…
ceremony is a child's hand…
reaching for a flower…
ceremony is the shadow of her favorite plant…
dancing in the sun across her wall…
ceremony is opening her candle-lit entry to a calling guest…
ceremony…is every sound…
ceremony…is every movement of Life…
ceremony…is a drink of precious water…

Woman…ceremony beckons…as in the times of Old…
Life as ceremony…beckons…

Woman…
Listen…to hear the Ceremony of Life…
…to hear the very stones…
…to hear the unspeakable…the unheard…
…to hear Infinity's Call…

Remember…the music of the spheres…

Attachments my dear woman-child…
keep you from the very songs of heaven's door…
from the very sounds of Creation…
from your Heart's Call…
The building pressure you feel within…
is your very own Self…wanting to Be…

Your very desire to Be…
shall open wide the doors…
perhaps slowly…a little glimpse at a time…at first…
that you may gain a footing…
and don't disgrace your dance…

You Woman…are Love…are Grace…are Beauty-SHE…
of all the fairy tales…
waiting to Be…

The waiting part is over…
History…alone is complete…
It is awaiting HERstory…
It is Time…
Now is the Time…
awa tey ewa tey
Now is the Time…

Gather ye with like-minded ones…
Your rememberings will spark and kindle
other rememberings…

And go ye alone into the Vastness of your Self…
Enter the invisible realms…to Know…

How…you say…
Go into the ONEness…
Go unto the Creator…
Go alone…
Be not afraid to be solitary
for in solitude with the ONE…
will you find the Many…
ONE and the Many…
ONE and the same…

Woman…in your solitude
you will find your magnet
deep within your Soul…

You will find your magnet
that will attract unto you
all that you need…
with no thought…
just simple Knowing…

In your solitude…
you will Know with whom to gather…
you will Remember…

Man-world may well be offended by some of this message…
But archetypal-Man will not…
for he knows, remembers and awaits…
the coming of True Woman…

HE awaits…to Behold the Beauty…
He awaits…to enter…her runway to Infinity…
He awaits…their journeys together unto the many mansions…
He awaits…with great expectancy…

HE…it is…who has awaited woman's true place
as an equal by his side…
to share in balanced measure…that which SHE brings…

What SHE…brings to HE…
unto these times…
is non-time…the NOW…
the ability of changing woman…
to merge with all…
the dance of LOVE…

Remember this song…from past the sky…
"I AM Infinity…play through me"…

Remember…who you are…
and let us…journey on…

And SHE…it is…who remembers how to hear the OWL…
to Know owl as instrument of Spirit…
speaking through whatever guise it takes
to Remember…that *I AM ONE*…

And SHE…it is…who remembers her wings…
soaring through the sky…
feeling the energies extend
to the farthest reaches of Creation…
And on the wings…
comes the remembering of the Sacred Union…
when Sky enters the crown…
and Earth enters the feet…

And together…they merge in the Heart…
remembering only LOVE…
full and complete…
Wholeness already is!

We are only remembering…
and the Earth is Already Saved…

Wholeness is…
and Wholeness beckons…
Its call…is the door into the magical
Land of the NOW…
the ONCE upon a non-time…
beyond all time and space…
known by each…in the ONE-Soul…

Come…it is time…

*Journey-SHE…
from the Stars unto the Stones…*

A Journey from the Stars unto the Stones

Introduction

This story came to me pre-dawn on July 14, 1989. The sound Sheoekah Amu had already been coming to me for several years, always as I was painting Soul images from the inner realms. Images of the Archetypal Dance...of the ONE as the Sacred Two...the ONE...as HE and SHE.

Sheoekah is a sound which to me means SHE...of...the...Heart. Amu is a sound that has Lemurian rememberings...of a time of mergings...flowings...blendings...of all forms. Sheoekah Amu is a sound with which my Soul resonates. It is a sound that speaks to my heart. When one goes to the Center of one's Being and there finds a sound, not a word or a name, but a sound... that most feels like one's inner-most Self...one is closer...ever closer to knowing and experiencing the true nature of one's Being. This sound came to me after many years of making Soul tones and sounds in sacred ceremony.

Sounds and tones began to come to me in 1975, during the painless birth of my second daughter. The painlessness was totally due to the sounds from the void. It was as if I were merged with a sound ray, which sounded and moved me simultaneously. It is a "sacred birthing dance" that is known by the feminine of both Man and Woman. The birthing dance happened through me...as I allowed!

The Soul tones and sounds have continued. They have facilitated the opening of my inner vision, my Soul songs, my rememberings, my ceremonial dances, my Soul mudras. I currently translate or interpret those rememberings in my paintings, sculptures and ceremonies! We can each bring forth a Remembering of…the Garden! It has never left.

It is only we…sweet ones…who fell asleep and forgot.

I say…Let us…Remember…
Now…Let us Remember…
It is time…

And then, much later, on the day of Chernobyl, in Russia, when the nuclear plant exploded, planet Earth was exposed once again to fission, rather than fusion. It is, indeed, unfortunate that as a people we create openings and changes through explosions and fission (separation), rather than mergings, fusion…Love. As a people, we will create whatever we need to experience, in order to learn. So without consciously knowing the Chernobyl tragedy was even happening, I felt an energy. It was as if a huge chasm was created in the collective mind. I knew that day that I needed to either create a strong outer distraction for the day or go into deep meditation or I would go into a deep depression, for I merge easily! I chose meditation and sat in contemplation of the ONE all day.

Late in the afternoon, my inner vision opened, larger than ever before. My home planet and part of my mission/purpose… opened before me…revealed.! I saw seven beings of Light…my Soul mission group…and I experienced ecstasy of pure Light.

And I remembered!

I say…WE NEED NOT CREATE Chernobyls, Challengers,

famines, over-populations, pollution, crime, a broken ecosystem…to blast us to change. To create openings that send shock waves around the globe…that we either "go under" or "go through." Transcendence…illumination…need not be painful!

Let us now collectively...in ever larger numbers...choose to Remember!
Let us allow together the free flow of the ONE to pour through us.
Let us create openings in a more organic gentle fashion!
Let us create a painless birth!

I offer this story...
A Journey from the Stars unto the Stones...
as a gift to reinspire others to Remember...
to Remember who they really are and
why they are here...

And when we Remember...if even just a glimpse...
our consciousness and thus our minds and bodies...
our Temple Template of Infinity...will fill with Light...
...with ecstasies, unspeakable...and we will KNOW!

For it is Time...

A Journey from the Stars unto the Stones

My name beith…Sheoekah Amu…
and I have a Story to tell…
I have come a journey…
from the stars unto the stones…
And you shall know me henceforth
as Sheoekah…
The Story I have to tell…
it beith a great Story…
A TRUE Story…the Great TruStory…
HIS-story…as it were…without HER-story
has been lacking…indeed…
But the Time, as we all know, has come
in the Story…
to add herstory to history…
to gather in the True Story…
henceforth known as the Trustory…
And so it is that the True Story begins…
Let us begin then…
With Once Upon a Non-Time…
a non-time…a non-time…a non-time…
beyond all time and space…
I remember…I remember…I remember…

I remember who I AM…
and I AM SHE…
SHE…it is…I AM…
And I am come…seeking HE…
HE and SHE are ONE
for there is only ONE…
ONE…the Undivided…

shooting forth...as it were...
unto Creation's Story...
Now...the divided...
HE and SHE...
The Divided...as it were...
ever seeking to reunite...
HE and SHE...alone in this grand universe
ever seeking to unite...
It beith ever...an electrically sexed universe...
regardless of the electromagnetic names,
pondered...as it were...
by science and the ever human mind...

Let us enter a field beyond the mind...

For many there are upon this little planet...
the one you know as Earth...
who Be...Landing...
And many there are
who Be...Taking off...

I beith...as it were...One who is Landing...
and you shall know me henceforth
as Sheoekah...
Sheoekah Amu...I Am...
It would seem upon your time,
that I telleth a personal story...
That is only a seeming...
The True Story...the Trustory...
is indeed an Impersonal Story...
Be not deceived by the personal seemings
or you shall miss the great unmasqueing...
We are all being prepared for a Grand Unmasqueing...
and Grand it shall Be...

Ancient Beauty…as it were…
shall pour over the land…
ancient, aboriginal, primal beauty…
Beauty that shall stop the Mind…
And so it is that Beauty-SHE of all the fairy tales…
shall spread upon the land…
And SHE…shall prepare the mortal mind
to enter into non-time…

And so it is…
Once Upon a Non-Time…
beyond all Time and Space…
and the Story begins…
The True Story…the Trustory
The Story of HE and SHE…
All the fairy tales are true
and legend upon legend
in the grand scheme of things
has kept the magic alive…

There beith across the lands and across the seas at this time…
great blendings…
They shall be known henceforth as…
The Great Blendings…
Ethnic Blendings and bleed-throughs
from all cultures and from all time…
Beauty from all pastime…blended into the Now…
Beauty of unprecedented splendor shall flow across the land…
And it shall be Holy…
it shall be sanctified…
for it is Beauty's preparation for the Great Wedding…
the Great Unmasqueing…
when all shall bare their souls…

Together, as it were, we prepare for the Wedding Feast...
when the Many of the One...
reveal the great Revelation of all time...
There is only One Soul...only One Mind...
that together...we are that One...
amen...and amen...
Woman shall henceforth be known as Beauty-SHE...
for SHE... it is...in all you know as men and women...
who prepares the WAY for the Great Wedding
and prepare SHE shall...
All the kingdoms of the Mother bow to HER
as SHE begins now...to gather the flowers for the wedding...

For this Journey from the Stars unto the Stones...
is preparation for the Holy Wedding...
the sky shall marry unto the earth...
the dusk conceives the night...
the dawn conceives the day...
Primordial's Beauty has always been with us...
only now are we prepared to see...to Be...

We enter...as it were...
unto a time of Holy Ceremony...
Sacred Ceremony...Living Ceremony...
Each moment...as it were...never to be repeated again...
for we prepare for a time of always new...
always Now...
No-thing ever to be reproduced, cloned, copied,
rehearsed or lived again...

The Holy Gift of Living Ceremony is...
as it were...The Great Marriage...
The Alabaster Marriage...
And...so it is...

*Native-HE…dances with birds…
and flies over the glowing lands…*

Galactic Shamanism

Galactic Shamanism is the mysticism of Balance…
when sky marries earth…
Spirit enters matter…
Father embraces Mother…
man and woman unite as One…

Galactic Shamanism is…
when day kisses night…and there is DAWN…
when night kisses day…and there is DUSK…
when past and future merge and…
Ceremony in the NOW…the Present…
only to present the gift (present)…
of the knowledge of the kingdom of NOW…

Galactic Shamanism is the Aboriginal Dreamtime…
held in sacred trust by Australian aboriginals…
a time that to them refers to the origins of Life
and its link into the future…

NOW is the Time…
in His-Story (history) when a new URN…is being formed.
It is a Cosmic Urn
where shards of Her-Story from non-time
are added to His-Story to create the True Story…
a Trustory…a new adventure for us all…

NOW is the Time…
of awakening to the Kingdoms of the Mother…
Ancient Earth-Mother is reflecting Christ
in mineral, plant and animal kingdoms…
The Revelations are HERE as we go

to the loudest concert of them all...
SILENCE...

NOW is the Time...
when Feminine Principle accesses
Cosmic Cauldron, the seemingly impenetrable
black hole, to pour forth the image
and likeness of the ONE Creative Mind...
and to learn that the Truth is..."Believing, thus seeing,"
rather than the other way around...

NOW is the Time...
for essence to expose Herself...naked...
as the Birther of New Forms...
Just imagine..."once upon a non-time"...
and enter the ecstatic vertical orgasms
of the new fairy tales of the Kingdom of NOW...

Starry Mantle of Spirit

Message from Spotted Owl

I come unto you in the night, O child...
I AM OWL...
I AM Spotted Owl...
I no longer can co-exist on this dimension
with free will choices as they are...
I am a most sensitive creature...
I am making my last plea to be heard
upon this physical plane of existence...
If my call is not heeded...
I shall move on...as have other species...
Help to make my plea heard....

Beseech others to go into Nature to hear me...
Beseech them to go into the Night...
Beseech them to communicate with me...
Tell them to Listen...Listen with their inner ears...
They shall hear me...
I have much to share with them...
Wisdom do I give unto their lives...

Tell them to Listen as a child...
Listen as a child would listen...
And they shall discover a new knowing...
a knowing of a new hearing...
an inner hearing...
If that should come, I would stay...
By invitation, of the human kingdom, I would stay...
En masse...they must wake...
They must awake...and hear our message

came pre-dawn April 19, 1991

Spotted Owl speaks here as the indicator species for the Ancient Forest.

The message from spotted owl was followed by a more personal message of one of the many gifts that spotted owl does bring.

Gift of Spotted Owl

O child...I can give the gift of sight...
clear-seeing...
clear-seeing...even unto the night...
I can see beyond deception and distortion...
I see clearly...
To see...is to know...
I can help one to see from the Center...
where All is visible...
from the Center of the Circle...
Call on me for sight...
Wisdom follows...

Spotted Owl Story

This poem and message came to me pre-dawn. They simply dropped powerfully into consciousness. I penned them both.

While showering that morning, I asked to know more about what had come and why it had come. There was an overlighting. It was both subtle and of great power.

I was shown that the Christ manifests in many forms. In this case, the Christ energy of Light has manifested as owl. Spotted owl.

I was guided to create a booth at the upcoming Earth Day Celebration of 1991. It was only three days away, on April 22.

Here is the story:

I will share some of the magic and synchronicities and co-incidents that emerged as I enacted each piece, as revealed.

I signed up to create a spotted owl booth at the Earth Day gathering. It was a daytime event. Later in the day, I was invited to do a presentation of the poem at the evening Earth Day program in the high school auditorium.

I said yes to presenting at both events. At the day event, I created a booth with a beautiful photo of spotted owl, kindly loaned by the U.S. Forest Service.

Note: Northern California has been losing much old growth forest to timber sales. Spotted owls are the indicator species for the well-being of the forests, so they have been protected.

Also in the booth were copies of the poem and the message from spotted owl. I handed those out.

I was inwardly guided to be neutral at the booth. To assist with that, I had a second paper to hand out that was a simple and neutral listing of what is needed for this indicator species in their habitats, the old growth forests.

The health of this species is a reflection of the health of the forest. And it is a reflection of us, humanity.

When inwardly guided to be neutral, I did not have anything "for or against" in the booth. I simply presented the habitat that was needed. I showed each person what was needed for the healthy environment. Each could draw their own conclusions.

A man arrived at the booth. He asked me whose booth it was. I indicated that it was my booth. He told me that he needed to go to his vehicle and get something and that he would return.

This man returned with a spotted owl feather. He then told the following story. He said he had been camping locally the night before. When he awoke in the morning he stepped outside his tent. Before him was a feather. A spotted owl feather. He picked up the feather. He was told from within that he would know to whom to gift the feather. He said he was told that it was not for him.

I was gifted the feather. It was a clear sign from the universe.

My long hair had a small braid beneath it. He positioned the feather in the braid. Clearly a gift from Great Spirit.

The evening enactment had its own story. I had called a local musician to see if he would play an earth rhythm on his drum, before and after I read the poem and message from spotted owl.

The musician relayed that he had been out walking in the forest earlier in the day and received a clear message that he would be playing at an event in the evening. When I called him, he knew immediately that this was the event.

I was shown not to be introduced or even announced. It was all created as a sacred enactment for spotted owl and the forest.

The drummer walked out on stage and quietly began a low, slow rhythmic drumming. I slowly walked on stage, dressed ceremoniously. I read the poem from spotted owl. I then walked silently off the stage. Drumming ensued for a short time. There was the same ceremonial cadence. Then silence.

The auditorium was stilled. Great silence prevailed.

Spotted owl's message was deeply heard.

We are all capable of being animal communicators. We may all be in deep communion with the soul of these beings. We may open to how to co-exist with the animals and be in inter-species communication, in a changing and emerging culture of beauty and harmony.

Later in this book, in Journey through the Kingdoms, is shown a very simply way to open to these communings. It is time that we all open to feeling and being one with our animal brothers and sisters.

This current of Life appearing is available to us all. May this story serve as inspiration to follow these ever present illumined threads before us.

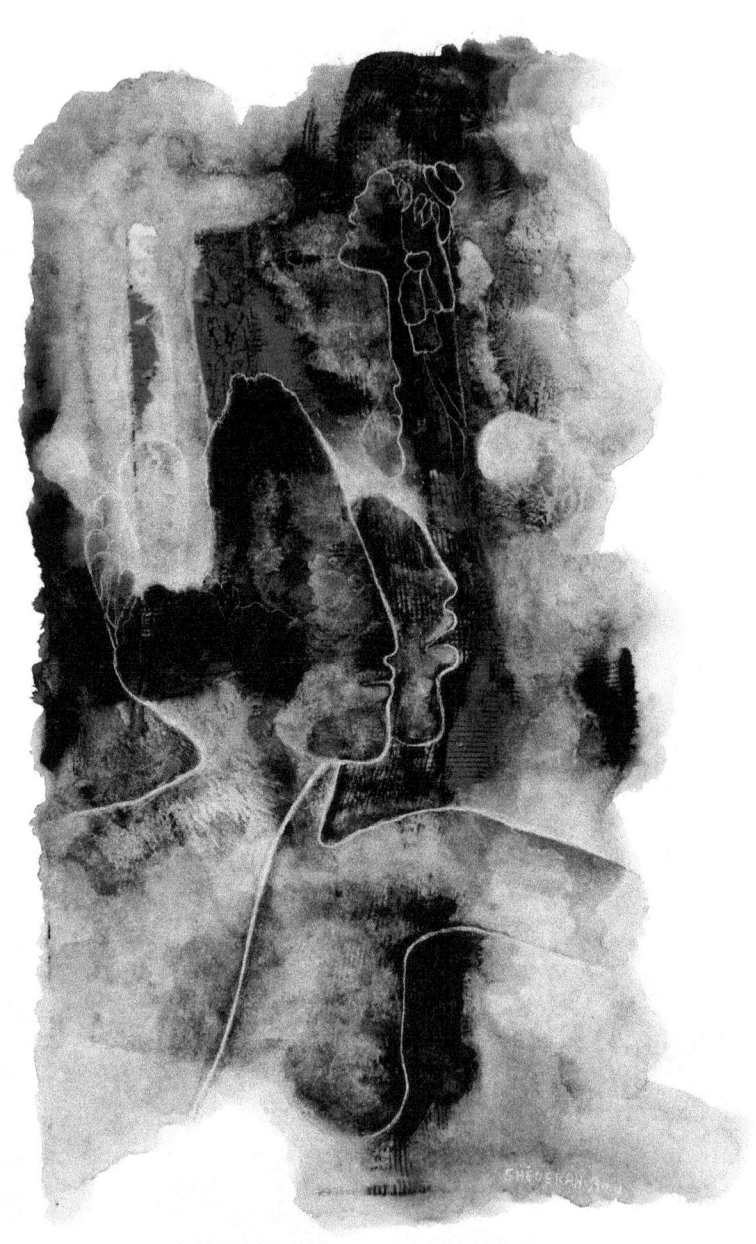

*and together…they dream and sing of worlds unseen…
and together…they build…
the royal twos…they build…
and the tribes…they land…
in the sacred two by twos…
they know well…and they remember…*

The Earth is Already Saved

It's already happened…
It's already here…

Open your eyes to behold…
Open your hearts to behold…
Open your minds to behold…

Leave behind the concept
so long lodged in the human mind
that there is a someone
or a something to save…

The Earth, my dear ones,
is already saved…
The kingdoms, my dear ones,
are already saved…

The last piece of this my mission,
to anchor in the star dome of Earth,
is to dislodge the concepts of the human mind
that would create the illusion of sickness…

Look not unto the appearances, my children…
Look deep into Reality…
Come with me deep within…and drink…

Drink of the nectar of Truth…
Drink of the picture that I shall reveal…
Drink…
Drink of God's pure Essence…

Then let that flow through your laser minds...
and create...
Allow me, the Father, the Almighty ONE...
finally to create...
in my very own image and likeness...

Close your eyes and see the Truth...

Allow heaven's door to open
and reveal my perfect world!
It already is!

The last to receive this message is the human mind, and man, who by my Grace, has received free will...has, by and large, chosen to function by free will, in separation, rather than live at one with the ONE mind, the ONE heart, the ONE soul...

Each human must, of its own accord,
align with the ONE Mind.
There is no battle;
there is nothing to save;
there is only, my children,
a free will choice of each human...

But, you say, the planet looks sick. Yes, the appearance is so.

You are so loved by the Creator, that HE has given a time lapse on this level of seeming reality, so you can see the reaction to your actions...and learn to make new, wiser choices.

The Earth can use her elements:
earth, air, fire and water
to rumble, shake, flood and burn...
to clean the disharmonic species from her cover.

And that she can do
and will do...
if the free will choice
to align the mind with Source, Spirit...is not made...

Yet even that has already happened.

Larger, ever large numbers,
are Remembering ME...
and by Remembering ME...the Father...
they will Remember the Mother...the Earth...
My Creation...

The Creator is manifest as Creation!

I can't be anything but whole and perfect.
Find the place in you where that is so.

Align your action with the vision of my wholeness...
Allow your actions to grow from the vision of wholeness...
Actions based on a vision of wholeness!

That is the Way, precious ONES.

On the Medicine Wheel...
take the wisdom of the Eastern race,
run through the mind of the Northern race,
acted on by the body of the Southern race
and felt by the heart of the Western race,
who have anchored in the care of the Earth,
the interrelatedness and interconnectedness of the Earth.

We need the tools of all the races
to build my vision on Planet Earth...

Let us begin this day...
Let us realign our minds to the wholeness...
that already is!
Let us begin to build this day...

Let us find ways...new ways...to reinspire our brothers and sisters...to realign their vision with wholeness that their lives will finally, after eons in spiritual darkness, begin to reflect my wholeness...and that the Revelations can begin, perhaps first as glimpses, then ever greater can the veils be dropped, the Truth exposed...that I...already AM.

ONEness...already IS...for those who KNOW...

Find that KNOWing,
in your heart
and in your Soul...
Judge no longer by appearances...
Live out your life from the inner vision of Wholeness...

Believe no man...
go within and find revealed this Truth
of Wholeness and Perfection...

I AM...the ONE...

So you see, the Earth is already saved.
She is dirty...it is true...
but she of her own accord will remedy that,
if her caretakers, her guardians, the human race,
do not in large numbers begin to realign
their single, individual minds to the ONE Mind,
to Source...and fulfill their function.

The human is the only form on the planet given the free will that allows it to deviate from Wholeness…

All else…is connected to the ONE Plan…
All else…waits for human mind to come
humbly…back to the ONE…

came pre-dawn on February 14, 1992, Valentine's Day

Part Three:
Awareness from the Invisible Realms

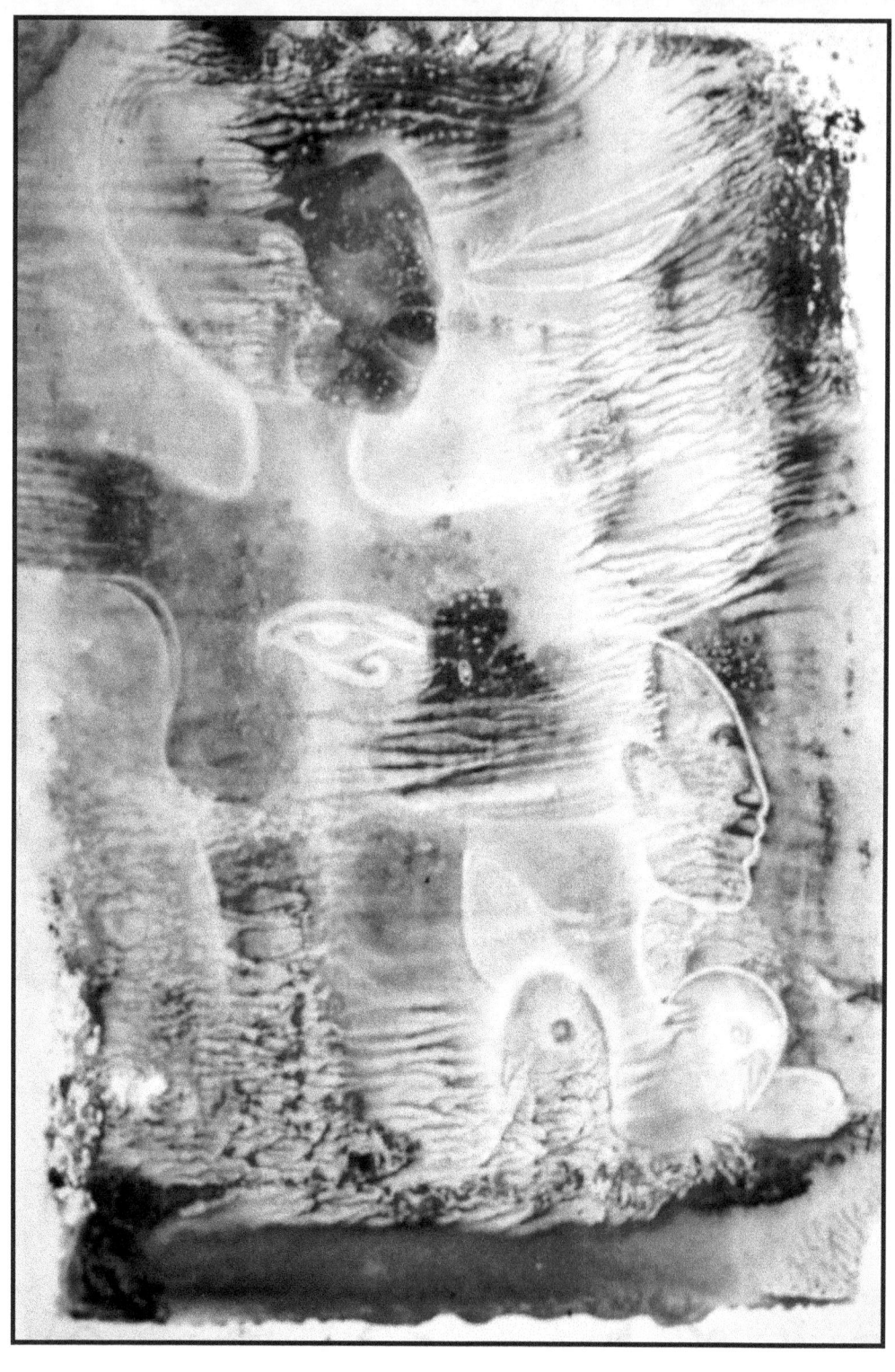

Beauty-SHE and HE…Embraced by the Universe

Galactic Shamanism Journeys

Journey through the Kingdoms and the Elements

As more and more people awaken, we hear of ones who have had both small and immense glimpses of a world beyond this appearance world. The Essence world. Even those with near-death experiences return to tell us of the seemingly Invisible world of Spirit.

We may all begin to see that the expanded and higher Consciousness is Already Here. It has never left. And we may open to its preciousness now. It is we that come and go, in human consciousness, getting peaks experiences, glimpses, signs and some synchronicities and co-incidents.

As we open and meditate on Source, the open doors to the Invisible reveal themselves in many ways. And often when we least expect it. It may come in many guises. This dying to the world of the seen allows the doors to the kingdom to be seen as open.

Ultimately, we quit coming and going in the human mind and we abide in Divine Mind, not as a glimpse, but as Life itself. We dwell in the Sublime. The very presence of God. Simple joys appear!

This practice of Journey through the Kingdoms and Journey through the Elements provides a subtle and uplifted passage into the Essence World. That which the world calls magic and mystical. This allows the unveiling of the mystical.

In that, we have an opportunity to simply Be in the Essence World. The seeming separation between physical and non-physical does begin to dissolve. The sense of separation between the visible and Invisible does flee. And the seen and Unseen… One.

Introduction to the Journeys

Following are sacred practices that I have used with myself, individuals and small groups since the 1970s. Ones began to come to me after I had a near-death collision in 1971 and I opened to the soul realm of Life. I opened to the joy of it. Many people from across the nation and around the globe have traveled with me on this Odyssey of Oneness. I have guided many both indoors and out in Nature on these journeys. It has been ecstatic. And revelatory. I am in gratitude for all that I have learned and experienced.

I now offer these practices in this new edition of the book, in written form, that more may benefit from them. They came to me over time and much at-one-ment practice.

Shared here is a way one may initiate himself or herself into these journeys, these odysseys into non-time, a realm that humanity is beginning to open to and explore. It is, indeed, an adventure that allows for an expansion of consciousness. It may seem magical and mysterious, but that is just a seeming. It is natural. It is where the so called visible and invisible do meet. And the ordinary and extraordinary. The natural and supernatural. This is a wondrous adventure and worth beginning.

Here lies the consciousness of a world often forgotten by humanity.

Here lies the awareness of the ever-present and every-where presence of Light.

Here lies the experience of feeling and knowing.

The experiences of doing these practices may change how one feels and experiences the so-called outer and physical world.

One does not need to be a scientist or a quantum physicist to open this door. Even children may play here.

These sacred practices are communions with the natural world. They are alignments with the laws of balance which are the laws of love. These sacred practices are not engaged in for psychic reasons. It is not for control. This is not for the superficial reason of more phenomena.

These communings are practiced and lived for the purpose of enriching one's life to include experiencing the Soul realm. The essence realm. The Christ. The presence of Life.

These communing practices are for those who want to deepen and expand their experience with everyone, everything and everyplace. They are for those who want to deepen in living… As the One.

These practices are to deepen our sensitivity and communication with all of Nature. To feel. They are to deepen our honoring and respecting of all of Nature. They call for reverence of this Earth, this environment, on which we live. That is what we have been given. The Earth. A holy environment.

There are, of course, many ways to attain this deepening.

I offer this way, as it was given to me.

On this Journey of Light may be experienced the Oneness that we Already Are. Light is a carrier of Love and Wisdom, so these are also powerfully experienced as a part of the environment we live in.

As well, messages and communications from the kingdoms and the elements may come. Sometimes these messages are greatly instructive. Other times they are warnings to the individual about the life choices and the lifestyle. Sometimes it is simply for the sheer joy of communing. Like child's play. Other times they are indicators of the way humanity must self-direct itself to divert needless disasters.

Almost all of the ones that I have navigated through the Journey of Light have had uplifting and heavenly experiences. Only a very few did not want to hear portents, regarding the plea from the animals, plants or the elements. Those warnings are a call for change. Individually and globally. There are still ones who resist change in life on planet Earth, as we have known it. It is a choice.

In navigating this realm, one must release beliefs about what we think reality is. Remember that many of Earth's creatures may see, hear and sense far beyond what humans have opened to.

Navigating through new and illumined realms expands our experience upon this plane of existence. It is a bringer of joy. Rapture even. And great Intelligence unfolding. Epiphanies.

This expansion of human consciousness to higher Consciousness allows us to have openings into another higher potential. Another world. These short or long glimpses may be life changing in our experience of Being Here Now.

They may elevate us enough to see that we are being shown "previews of potential coming attractions" on planet Earth. And I speak not of the movie theatre and films called fantasy. I speak of the Oneness of the so-called mundane and supra-mundane. I speak of seeing through the eyes of the Soul. Seeing directly the illumined world that IS, if we have eyes to see.

I will share an experience I had with a friend around 2013-14. My friend and I had hiked numerous times. This time we chose to hike in to a waterfall. When we arrived to this sacred space in Nature, I suggested we both go off alone and be still for some time. The plan was to come back to the same spot and enjoy our sack lunches together on the rocks.

When my friend arrived back after some time, we ate and talked and fell into deep appreciation of this sublime and pristine environment that appeared to be singing songs from everywhere. At one point, my friend mentioned she had pain in her shoulder. I invited her to close her eyes. I told her I would do a meditation for her, holding space for her Wholeness that Already Is.

I could feel the growing energy that was pouring in from "above." I finally asked my friend if she could feel it. She could. I suggested we keep our eyes closed longer and continue to open to this amazing infusion of Light. I finally opened my eyes. Initially, I was almost shocked. I just continued to hold space in the divine light of Being.

Following is what I witnessed.

Everything in the environment was luminous, glowing. It was unearthly. The waterfall, the pool of water below, the rocks and foliage everywhere. All of it was fully illumined. It seemed impossible for Nature to be both Nature, as we have known it, and effervescing as Light, as well.

It outdid all the film special effects I have ever seen in films. This was the movie screen we call life.

I asked my friend to slowly and gently open her eyes and tell me what she saw. She saw the identical environment. I suggested that we stay very still and stay centered in the Light, and just take in this "Heaven AS Earth," this experience of numina.

We simply sat there in the splendor revealed.

It began to fade slowly during our hike back to our cars. But the level of elevation of feeling lasted for both of us into the evening hours.

No, there were no drugs or psychedelic plants in this experience.

And why am I sharing such a personal story? I feel that it is our story. Humanity's story. It is a part of a way greater Impersonal Story. A Divine story. That story includes everyone, everything and everyplace. It is inclusive. The One Story.

And I feel that these Journeys through the Kingdoms and Journeys through the Elements may assist and hasten the global shift. The awakening to the true and essential nature of all. And they may awaken us to the true nature of our relationship with all the Earth.

We are opening to the soul of everyone, everything and everyplace. No more will we need to malpractice in our lives. We may see to the inner core of light. We may begin to see beyond appearances.

These practices may be done alone or you may assist another by being the facilitator.

The depth of experience depends strongly on one's depth of awareness.

Important points:

1) Whether guiding yourself or another, one must be aligned with Source/Divine Mind. The presence of God. Christ. Use whatever form of meditation or attunement (at-one-ment) works best for you. Listen within.

Note: At the back of the book, one may find information about my meditation CD, *Journey of Consciousness,* which is available.

2) It is important to note that this practice is facilitating an opening to more of the Infinite Love and Intelligence. It cannot be used for psychic reason or to control or manipulate in any way.

3) This is a time to practice being yin, the feminine principle, of our expression. Be receptive. Open. Allowing. Be the witness. The observer.

4) It is equally important that there be a sincerity and an earnestness about Awareness of the One. In that, Nature is The Sanctuary and we enter with reverence. Pure intentions. Purity is a key.

5) We must release limitations in the form of beliefs and judgments. Be aware that we enter in consciousness, here and now, the new earth culture. Rise above the sense or belief in duality.

6) Create a sacred space indoors or choose a space out of doors that will be perfect and conducive for this odyssey. Keep in mind possibilities like candles, silence and deep reverence for the divine nature of all of life.

We will Journey through the Kingdoms: mineral, plant, animal, nature spirits and angelic being.

Let us begin.

Journey through the Kingdoms

Note: These guidelines are loose in that you are being spontaneous and trusting. Allow all to be seen as liquid light and flow with it.

Note to facilitators: You must be able to hold sacred space in the Light of Being for the other person. You are aware of them with your sacred vision. You are aware of them as their true nature. Illumined Wholeness. The Christ of God.

Do not focus on the personality or interfere in anyway with the person's unique inner journey.

Those wanting more information of how to do this may read my book *The Holy Sight*. The subject is covered in depth.

1) It is best to do this practice while sitting. In lying down, it is too easy to drift off, as we are in very subtle realms of expressions. Ineffable. Then close the eyes and be comfortable.

2) Now do the deeper alignment with the One Presence (meditation) in the form that you are drawn naturally to. Feel it.

One possible form is practicing the God Breath, Holy Breath of the ever present presence through every cell in the body. Feel the Light of Being on the inhale into the heart. Hold it until it naturally wants to release. On the exhale, allow all that Light to radiate like an expanding sun through and around and as every cell in your body. Feel it. Feel your Body of Light.

Do this for several breaths, all the while opening and feeling. Being. Be receptive. The Lover and Beloved as One.

Then sit for a while in this stillness, allowing a deepening. There is generally a feeling of "I am ready."

3) Now, with eyes still closed, gaze upon the precious Earth, with inner vision. Scan her slowly and carefully. Allow yourself to see her glowing as a star. See her illumined nature of wholeness and perfection.

Now using your intuition, allow yourself to find a place on the Earth for this experience. Choose a place that most deeply resonates. It can be anywhere. Indoors or out of doors. On water or land. Be careful not to be mental about this. Allow inner knowing to guide to the perfect location on this planet.

Take whatever time is needed. One will feel it.

4) Once you are at the guided location, be aware that this first focus is on the mineral kingdom. Be fully free and without limitation. In this inner envisioning, you may be standing or walking or running, or whatever is guided.

5) Begin to look for something in the mineral kingdom. It will be something that you are naturally drawn to. It could be a rock, a boulder, a mountain, a pebble, a crystal. Allow your luminous body of Light to feel. Feel what you are attracted to. Trust.

Again, take whatever time is needed.

If you are guiding someone, be sure to have them tell or signal you when they have found their special mineral.

6) The next step is KEY.

Allow oneself to deeply feel and know of one's own Christ Light.

See and feel its emanations on out into the space around you. Breathe and feel the radiance. Be grateful. Breathe several more times in the same way. Drop into the deep space of peace. Allow the world, your life, your seeming problems and challenges, your concerns, to just fall away. For the moment, simply die to the world.

Now observe your chosen mineral. Know that all is Life. All is breathing. Now begin to breathe with the mineral. Breathe together. In sync. As One.

As you continue to breathe with this mineral, see it breathe in the omnipresent Light that is everywhere. And see it begin to exhale the Light. Continue to do this until you are aware of the mineral as illumined and glowing and radiating.

Like you, it has a radiant auric field of light around it.

In other books and later in this one, I have shared more about my 1971 car collision. At the moment that another car in the snow went out of control, I said, "God, I am yours." Then the crash. It is a much longer story, but what I want to share now is that after the crash, I could see the field of light (aura) around all living things. In fact, it was so strong that I was compelled to.

7) The next step increases the subtlety, so is also KEY.

Find an initial and natural way to approach this mineral. You and it are unique. You have a dance to do together. Allow the form of the approach to be very individual. No limitations. Allow this form to be very free and flowing, knowing this is an energy universe that flows. Changing. Forming. Reforming.

Think of water as it warms, freezes, evaporates and precipitates.

Next, notice your auric field (your emanating field of light. And witness the same with the mineral.

Then allow this next part of the practice.

Allow your auric field and its auric field to merge. To be at One. Feel it. Be in appreciation. Let the rest of the world just fall away. Allow the full expression of this focus.

8) This next part of the journey may seem utterly fantastic. Be willing to go with it. The Soul may speak to us via so many forms.

Allow creativity from Creator/Source to be upon you.

Allow the fullness of this experience to be revealed.

Let go of all concepts and opinions of what this should look like.

Trust what comes. Trust what is being shown to you.

Everyone that I have worked with has had totally different experiences. No comparisons here. I have seen many be led in their lives in such wondrous ways, via this practice.

It is the practice also of…everything is possible.

Allow whatever time is needed here. No need to hurry.

If you are facilitating another, hold deep sacred vision for the person in the inner journey.

And remember, it is always a journey that relates to the outer journey.

Now…create a deep relationship with this mineral. Allow what you are feeling to be revealed. Trust yourself, no matter how "crazy or fantastic" it may seem. (Remember the Wright brothers?)

One may become the mineral. One may enter the mineral. One may go on a flight with this mineral to another star. The possibilities are endless.

You may create a ceremony around the mineral or with it. You may climb on it or under it.

Allow what comes. Trust yourself. Experience fully. Allow yourself free reign.

Take whatever time is needed.

If you are facilitating another, have the other person to signal you when they are complete with this.

Know that some people take more time. There is no right or wrong time element here.

9) At this point in the inward odyssey, see if there is something that you wish to say or communicate to the mineral. Or you may ask if it has a further communication or message for you.

You may ask it any question that comes to you. It may be more personal, about your own life. Or it may have a message that humanity needs to know. And, right now, you are the receptive conduit for that message.

Get very silent. Listen. Gently listen inwardly. Take the time that is needed.

If you are guiding another, have them signal you when complete. And upon completion, they may share their full experience. I have found that they may share the experience more fully if they continue to keep their eyes closed.

Have them talk about any thing in the experience that relates to their life. Or the world.

10) When ready, open your eyes. Take the time to write down key things that happened or were revealed.

All of the Kingdoms will be re-viewed at the end to see any co-incidents, synchronicities.

Above are the ten simple steps to be taken for all of the Kingdoms.

***Continue to go through the same guidance as above with the other kingdoms: plant, animal, nature spirits, and angel selves.

I have found that the Journey through the Kingdoms may easily take from two to four hours. Give oneself plenty of time and space for this practice. Being "in time" is counterproductive to this unfolding awareness.

Journey through the Elements

The elements, earth, air, fire, water and ethers, may also reveal much Divine Intelligence.

Let us now attune to them and see them as the sacred manifestations of the divine that they are.

Let us attune to them deeply. And be in deep gratitude for them.

***You may use the instructions and the previous ten steps to encounter the elements in a sacred way.

Again, let go of the world. Let go of beliefs and opinions. Let go of your concept of reality.

Know that everything manifests via consciousness. Allow yourself to be guided by the higher Consciousness. Call it God or by any name that most touches and inspires you.

Be at One. Be free. Allow.

Note: I have observed that the experiences with the Kingdoms may be both very playful and powerful. Sometimes the kingdoms or elements may present what needs to change in the world to be in balance with Nature. Sometimes they are powerful messengers of change.

Do one's best to go on these odysseys with no preferences, with no preconceptions and with utter openness. This is an opportunity to open to "what is."

Experience, realize, grow…

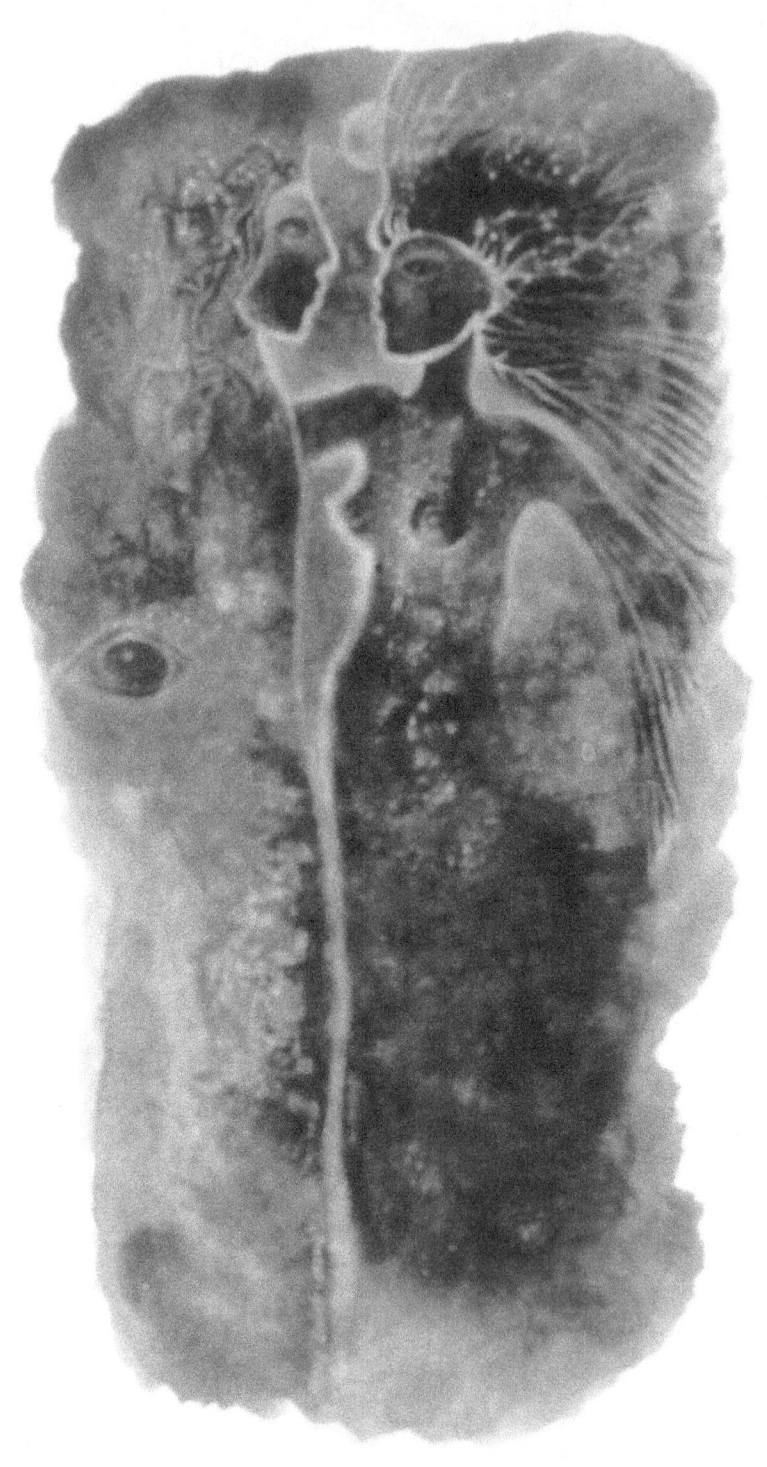

Changing Woman Star Dance

Teachings from Higher Dimensions and Original Archetypes Realms

Tapping into the non-dimensional, beyond the realm of time

Tapping into the Impersonal

Introduction

After my near-death car collision in 1971, described briefly in the section above, I began to have extraordinary experiences. I had now seen into the Unseen. I had experienced the soul realm of ecstasy. I had experienced the Time-less realm. I witnessed past, present, future of my life as One, in the instant of car impact. I had experienced rarified joy. I experienced my inner vision open. There was no turning back. There was no desire to turn back.

And I brought back with me from those experiences the ability to see the light around all living things. The aura. The precious field of light that surrounds us. I could see the light of being emanating. I was called. I was called by this Light of Being.

I had no idea that these experiences would continue. I did not know that one day I would see them as teachings for my life. Inner guidance. I did not ever dream that I would be sharing them with others. A friend had told me in the seventies that such illumined experiences should be sacred, secret, and silent. The friend said to not share them. And I read many times that these are simply phenomena.

So mostly, I stay sacred, secret, and silent with the inner revelations and treasures. They did appear and translate as art, poetry, sculpting, multi-media presentations, and in my spiritual education with others. The art became Art of the Soul. Soul Expressions. The experiences began to also find their way into my Soul Sessions and Soul Retreats with individuals and small groups. I found that they served as springboards of such beauty to inspire attunement to the divine for the seeming others.

I was acutely aware that each experience was a sacred gift in my life. I did not know yet how much they would sculpt my life.

I had not studied Joseph Campbell. Nor Carl Jung. Nor had I studied the Feminine Archetypes at that time.

My life was very simple. I was raising two young and precious daughters. I was creating very simple soul drawings in pencil and pen and ink of the divine feminine in all of my free time. (See my book, *Art As Consciousness*.)

I was living a life that was a strange mix of going out dancing, coordinating spiritual gatherings, concerts, and speakers, and being very silent and solitary. And I was learning slowly to dedicate my life to Spirit. I learned through a very bumpy ride that it included every aspect of my life. Sometimes I would wonder if I was a wild dancer; other times I would wonder if I was best as a monk. I loved both. And then they merged. I began temple dancing. Sacred postures, gestures, mudras. Soul glyphs. That is a long story for another time. (I share Temple Dancing workshops.)

All of my reading and spiritual studies, after the near-death experience of awakening in the Soul Realm and seeing my past, present, and future as One, continued to help in keeping the door open to the seeming Invisible dimensions. I now knew they were full of teachings that could assist me in living a consecrated life. I now knew clearly that there was a state of consciousness higher than the one that humanity both believes in and lives.

I now had a glimpse of Direct Knowing. There were no doubts that higher Consciousness exists. Direct experience had also revealed the simple joy and rapture of that realm. It could be called cosmic orgasm. Only it does not have to end. It is our home. True Home. And when it is experienced, it needs no introduction. It feels more real than what we regard as real. I began to call it The Realm of the Real.

From my reading, studies, contemplation, I clearly saw that I needed to learn how to stay in that sacred inner connection. I needed to learn to stay attuned to the presence of God, no matter the situation. Challenges surely present themselves in life. And many were presented to me. I did well in some. Not so well in others. Most important, I did not quit choosing to stay attuned and at One with the Oneness that IS.

It is clear that "Heaven AS Earth" is the calling and the challenge from the Infinite for all. It is clear that we need to practice the "heaven-world" Consciousness as a way of life.

> *As I share the teachings that have come to me from the original archetypal realms and dimensions, I must say how important it is "not to try to have these experiences."*
>
> *Never do I "try" to control or manipulate what is given to me when I become empty, let go of the world, and go into the Silence.*

Each of us is fully unique and individual, as a snow flake and all other expressions, and getting empty allows us to open to who we are and why we are here. It is important that we allow our own Soul Expression to surface and be lived. The great mystery of who we are surfaces. A mystery no more. And epiphanies come. And revelations.

These teachings that I share are helpful tools in relating to the divine and to our lives. They share of the Mystical as the Practical.

As you spend more and more time in the Divine Emptiness that is the Fullness, your life may unfold through you as a flowing current and expression that you may trust.

Below are the Teachings as given to me:

I have waited forty-five years to share more in depth about these direct experiences that have come to me. They are profound teachings that may fully change us. They certainly were direct revelation for me. And they changed me.

As I mentioned above, I have more indirectly shared these teachings through my art, sculpture, soul sounding, theater, poetry, poetic odysseys, writings, multi-media sacred enactments, Soul Sessions, The Holy Sight workshops, and spiritual retreats.

In Soul Sessions, the experiences from these archetypal realms and dimensions were often called forth for me to share, if it was known to be elevating for the person. When I began, in earnest, sharing the Soul Sessions in 1985, I found myself sharing from those pools of wisdom that arose unexpectedly from within.

I share them now, because I see the wisdom and teachings flowing from each of them.

I clearly see that they each came as guidance on my life journey. I share them now, not because I feel they are your personal journey, but because I feel that the wisdom gained is Impersonal and may benefit and elevate anyone. I have witnessed the teachings uplift large numbers of people in Soul Sessions.

I am very adamant about my next point.

I do not believe that we are here to focus on realms and dimensions. We are here to attune to the One, the Eternal, the presence of God, by whatever name. We are here for Realization of that One. And it is non-dimensional. Abide there. This is how we come to realize that I and the Eternal are One. We realize our Spiritual Identity.

Awareness. We are to realize I Am Awareness. The non-dimensional is Cause. Go to Cause and the effects-world will harmonize and flow. This is key.

One need not try to control and manipulate the effects world of phenomena. The effects world then seems to be magic.

We are told again and yet again that the only true teacher is in our heart. If we stay true to this, we will have divine guidance. I have found this to be true.

Being a girl from rural Iowa, it was quite incomprehensible that my life would ever bloom in the form and with the experiences that I am sharing below. I never imagined inner teachings and guidance in such unusual forms.

I offer now sixteen of the many inner-sight visions and teachings that have come upon me. It is my prayer that they be of deep upliftment into the heaven-world for others. May they serve as a prayer that initiates living in a higher frequency.

These experiences are tools and teachings that may help to live a life that is the Embodied Christ. The embodied Light of Being. When we do claim that and realize it, our human life shifts to a divine Life.

We realize that the glimpses into higher dimensions are revelations. We are the living revelations.

These experiences will mostly be shared in the order that they happened. I have been able to see that what looks like human timing and order is really Divine Order by the all-knowing Timelessness. I did not understand the timing for many decades.

>*Remember this: Each time I was attuning to the One! That is key.*

Below are the Teachings as given to me to experience and grow from.

The Realm of Pure Energy: Be Here Now (1971)

The Experience

Scientist friends gave me the book *Be Here Now,* by Ram Dass. As I began to read the unusual book, something began to radically shift in my entire being. I still do not have words to describe it well. My entire belief world seemed to be dissolving. And I resonated with the words. Such simple words…BE HERE NOW chimed through my very being. I was deeply moved on a cellular level even. My entire world seemed to be going through a crumbling and a re-orientation. So I continued to read it.

I read the book very slowly, taking it in deeply, eight times in a row. I would read, then re-read. At the end of the eighth reading, I simply entered another dimension. It included the living room in which I was sitting. I saw everything in the room as pure energy. I saw the world that I believed was so solid and physical was fluid, morphing energy. Nothing was solid or stable or unchanging, as I had been taught.

Currently we have many scientists and quantum physicists teaching how all of this works. They are bringing it to mainstream. Historically we have perceived the world in such a different way. We create structures, systems, institutions, governments, societies, and civilizations that are usually very rigid. They block and hinder the natural flow of the Universe. The very River of Life.

Perhaps we could come up with many reasons to dam the flow of that river. When we dam it, there is more opportunity to control and limit the world and people that are here. Creativity is curtailed.

It does seem that we are at a crucial and global denouement in humanity's journey of human consciousness to Divine Consciousness. It is a time, inculcated by the Timeless Realm, like no other in written history.

We find that we are not here to try to limit the Limitless One. We are here to align with it and flow with it. Allow it.

There is an awakening happening. But truly, we are just removing the seeming dams. Those dams are the sense of separation from Source. The belief in separation.

In the BE HERE NOW merging experience which I had, I and all that was with me in the room seemed to melt into pure energy. I was one with it all.

No, no drugs were involved.

This would be simply, "when the student is ready, the teacher appears." Why was I ready? I was suffering. Why was I suffering? I was a high school teacher. My husband was very successful in his engineer world. I had a healthy and absolutely awake and lively toddler. I knew something was missing. What? I had no idea.

Just this great emptiness within.

I had not even been praying for a change. I knew something needed to change. I was open to change. And change came.

The Teachings

1) Everything is fluid, morphing, and changing. It is not a static universe. Everything is liquid light.

2) The Changeless One brings the change.

3) Grace descends when we are open. However, it may not take the form we would necessarily want or even imagine.

Sky-Dancer SHE

The Soul Realm of Joy: Near-Death Experience (1971)

I want to begin by saying that I do not believe that suffering, disaster, disorder, pain, and fear are needed for the collective and/or individual awakening. However, it appears to be the way that much of humanity is awakening. And I have had my own share of disasters.

From the moment that we feel fear, in almost any form, we are in duality's drama and in the belief in separation from Source. There is no real separation from Source. It is a belief in separation and that is also a sense of separation.

Some people tell me it is a struggle or great work to stay out of that seeming separation. I respond by sharing that it is not nearly as hard as the pain, suffering, and consequences of staying in that belief.

And when one begins to practice Oneness Consciousness and begins to see synchronicities, flow, and harmony, then the desire to leave the belief in separation does greatly grow.

Some teachings say not to get stuck in stories. I fully agree. Yet throughout history, examples, parables, and stories have served soul growth for individuals.

This story is told only for the teaching. It may be useful to others in a number of ways.

The Experience

I was a college English instructor and I was driving to work.

This is during the period that I was very open to change. But, again, I did not see how to change. I had a daughter and myself to support.

I almost always drove the long way to work. I drove through beautiful rural Oregon on a dirt road. The quiet and beauty seemed to help prepare me for the day. I was living in an area that gets little snow, but lots of rain. And this a.m., it was snowing. I was not concerned. I lived and drove for many years in Iowa and Wisconsin storms and even blizzards.

I saw a car coming. As it neared me, I could see that it was going out of control in the snow. I would either need to turn left or right into deep ravine-like ditches. Or I would have a head-on collision. It was too slippery to throw on my brakes.

In an instant, I chose the head-on collision. In the very next moment, I tightened my hands on the steering wheel. It seemed like an involuntary response. And simultaneously, I said, "God, I'm yours."

In that instant of the impact, I seemed to go through an opening created through the literary classic *Finnegan's Wake,* by James Joyce, the literary giant known for stream-of-consciousness writing. (I had taught that classic over the years, so I was familiar with it, although it was almost meaningless to me and we teachers needed a synopsis to guide us.)

Finnigan's Wake seemed to provide a framework and an opening through which the near-death experience could happen. It was somehow a portal.

In that same instant of the impact, I found my human consciousness to be higher Consciousness. I could clearly see my past, present, and future as One. One seamless life. It was through the eyes of unadulterated joy. Virgin joy. It was ecstatic. It was Soul Joy.

I was totally immersed in Consciousness of the Timeless Realm. That was how I could see past, present, and future as One and as Here Now. Again, here was the Be Here Now message.

It was not such a pleasant experience to face the collision and the totaled cars. It was all a seeming disaster. I was not hurt in the least, nor was the other driver. Both cars were totaled.

And still, the near-death experience brought several more levels of change in my life. It was what catalyzed me to finally leave teaching and pursue my soul's dream of art. It had been calling for many years. A decade.

The Teachings

1) The Timeless Realm is real.

2) The Soul Realm is more real than what we call the physical world.

3) The Soul Realm is illumined and full of the deepest joy. Ecstasy.

4) The Soul Realm is outside of duality. There is no human concept of good or bad.

5) The Soul Realm of Light is the Be Here Now.

6) The Soul Realm is full of presents from Presence.

After the experience, I could/can see the Life Force around living things. It is especially easy to see it around trees at a certain time of the day.

I realized during the experience that I had another, quite different, life to lead.

7) The Soul Realm is Already Whole.

8) The Soul Realm is a state of consciousness. It took many years of Withinness and study to finally realize that.

The Cosmic Birthing Force: Birthing Experience (1975)

The Experience

I will begin with some words about my first birthing experience, so that this second one is comprehended fully. I was pregnant with my first child and was just naively trusting what the doctor told me. There was almost no preparation for this forthcoming hospital birth.

I was living in Madison, Wisconsin, and I was teaching high school English. Peers were also having children. We were all ignorant and naive about birthing. There were some Lamaze classes. That was pretty much it. None of my friends were breastfeeding and I wanted to.

The birthing day came. My husband was afraid to be at the birth. Ha. So was I. I was given a spinal injection to numb me and I was put on my back. There was no gravity at play. And my feet were high in stirrups like I was riding a horse upside down. It was an insane posture for birthing. And even though I was numb, the experience was devastating. The birthing pressure is immense and someone is telling you when to push. When not to push. I can understand why women around the world often die at these "events."

In 1975, I was pregnant again. I had already decided that I would never go through that hospital style birthing torture again. I decided to spend much time, during the nine months, going within, feeling the One Presence, feeling the peace that is within, attuning to the incoming soul and studying and learning about birth from every source I could find.

I read many books on pregnancy and home birthing. I found a superb mid-wife. And I found a doctor and his nurse-wife to assist me if I reverted to old paradigm birthing pains. They would be present also.

I had a forty-five minute painless birth. At home.

In my second experience of childbirth, I discovered that birthing is a cosmic event and process.

The woman must be peace-filled, surrendered to the Cosmic Force, and very intuitive to her body. She must be able to listen. To feel. If she is following "outer" orders, all that inner attunement is lost.

I had prepared my environment with the sounds of Yogananda chants. I had total quiet in my home. I had built up the pillows on my bed in such a fashion that I had created a gravity flow for the baby's landing. It was like a runway or a landing pad for the incoming soul.

I was at the grocery market that morning. All of a sudden, I simply knew. I knew the baby was coming. I knew I must walk home quickly. I immediately called the doctor and the nurse. They told me to call back in a few hours, to allow the labor to progress. I announced to them very strongly that if they did not come now that they would miss the birth. They came.

I called the mid-wife; she immediately came.

We were all gathered and the music was playing. I said that the baby was coming. I could feel the primal force. It had nothing to do with me or anyone else deciding. The doctor told me not to push yet, as he had not checked the dilation. I replied that I did not need to push. I informed him that it was simply happening on its own.

The doctor wanted to come forward to measure the dilation. I remember saying, "Don't come near me. Don't touch me." The words came out of me powerfully, with certainty. Even I was amazed.

The cosmic birthing force was moving through me and I could feel the primal birthing rite. It was both a passage for the baby and a life's passage for me.

My role was to allow. To witness. To be present.

Several times the intensity would start to be painful. Instead of moaning, crying, screaming, I began to sound what sounded like ancient, primordial birthing sounds. Although they came through me, they did not sound as if they were from me. At first I felt inhibited but the mid-wife began making loud sounds to remove my inhibition. It worked. I really opened and allowed. As long as I was allowing the sounds, the pain would subside and leave.

The sounds truly arrived from another realm. They were otherworldly. I felt taken to another realm when they were coming forth. I felt like they emanated from a place that we do not know.

As the crowning occurred, I announced, "Her name is Rebecca Rachel." And she arrived. Perfect! Whole! I had done no testing to know the gender ahead of time. And the name was not the one I had chosen.

I was in such joy and gratitude.

The Teachings

1) We live in an Intelligent Universe. It knows what it is doing if we don't block the perfection with beliefs.

2) Preparation is helpful, not only on the physical and mental realms, but also the psychological realm. I saw that most modern births are unnatural. They do not create a conducive environment.

Preparation allows us to practice being fully open and present and surrendered.

3) All of humanity must learn to attune to and listen to the Withinness. The teacher residing in the heart. Then our guidance may come in many ways. Intuition, ahas, glimpses, clues from Nature, a book, a phone call or friend. There may be an impulse. A thought. We must be aware and alert to know what it means. We go from "I don't know" to Direct Knowing, with no doubts.

4) Humanity's return to Oneness is important also as an attunement to the Earth and her wisdom.

5) We must discern what is the truth in our life. And trust. And act.

Inner Music Realms: Angelic, Celestial, and Music of the Spheres (1978 and on)

These realms are transcendent, and once one has opened to hearing them, one has an entirely different perspective on music in the world. It is not that one cannot enjoy the world music. It is simply that these frequencies bring on a form of rapture and exaltation. One grows more sensitive to any sounds.

Music of the Spheres (1978)

The Experience

It was in the late-seventies and I was doing my best to raise two precious daughters alone. I was given $100 a month by one of the fathers. I add this detail for a very important point. I did not have the extra finances to run off and sign up for all the spiritual workshops, conferences, and expos that were beginning to happen, during that radical period of awakening. So I made the decision to study, dedicate, contemplate, and meditate, and I asked to open to the One within. I asked to open to the True Teacher within the heart.

During this time, I had a boyfriend that lived out of town. I had driven, with my daughters, to spend some time with this man friend. I assumed that we were in a monogamous partnership. Soon after I arrived, he let me know that he had a second girlfriend.

That night, I decided I must fully let go. I went into my heart. I let go of all in the seen world. I aligned with the Christ.

Then, the music began. A beatific music of the spheres. I had no idea sound could ripple into the world with such elevated and gossamer frequencies. I allowed myself to simply be One with this sound. Gift of Sound. This sound from the Infinite was beyond being a healing balm. It emanated from a place that needs no healing. It carries no chords of disharmony. It carries no dis-cords. It is the sacred sound from a Realm of Wholeness. A realm beyond duality's beliefs in good and evil.

I was quickly moving beyond the drama of a seeming "love lost." I felt as if I was in the "land of love found." And it was a deeper love. An all-inclusive love.

I did not feel a need to go get an explanation or see if this man would change his mind. In fact, I had no need to look back at the previous relationship.

The Teachings

1) I was awakened to another gift that humans carry. We carry the ability to hear the unseen. We carry the ability to hear the inner music realms. We may hear beyond this seen world of form They are notes, chords in the Invisible world. Sacred.

2) I was awakened to cosmic sound as sublime. Ineffable. These rarified sounds may change one. One's sensitivity does expand. Certain things in the world feel coarse and unrefined. Sense of beauty heightens.

3) It is also notable that when one fully "lets go" of controlling the outer plane of existence, that assistance may come in the form of an embodied heaven-world. I understood the deeper meaning of letting go. It is a bringer of "as above, so below." I had no beliefs to block the beauty of the higher music. I could

clearly feel how it permeated my physical, mental, and emotional bodies. I experienced Transcendence.

I realized this was "a teaching" for everything one encounters in life. I realized it could be of assistance to all of humanity. When ones give up the belief that controlling and forcing and manipulating is "the way" to get what they want, then a spiral into a higher consciousness may ensue. I let go of any resistance.

Angelic Singing Realm
August 1987, Harmonic Convergence

Over the years, I have had the inner music realms reveal themselves many times. I did not intend to share a second of the many sacred sound experiences, but this one also has some powerful teachings that came to me. They are relevant on this collective journey of galactic shamanism.

The Experience

It was August of 1987, on Harmonic Convergence. A friend from out of the country was visiting to celebrate Harmonic Convergence. She was staying in the guest bedroom on the other side of my home.

For years I had been going outside each morning at early dawn. One of my spiritual practices was to do that. I would stand fully naked on the earth with bare feet, facing the mountain. I would do this in all weather…rain, wind, and snow. Then I would practice being fully transparent, illumined body. I would open to feel the breeze and wind through me. When I was done I would paint and sculpt. I did this much of eight years. It elevates the Soul.

So this August morning found me with naked feet on the precious earth. As the sky lighted it was filled with unusual clouds unlike any I had ever seen. They filled the sky. I was simply observing the unusual phenomena, when the sky began to "open." I could hear music pour in from the sky. There were words. It was voices, but not like human voices. Over and over, I began to hear angelic voices singing. These words did come: "I Am the Infinite. Play through me." I was already very open, so this angelic chant was taken in deeply in consciousness and on a cellular level. It was felt.

Then I remembered my sleeping guest. I ran into the house and down the hall and tried to wake up my friend, so that she could come outside. This friend immediately asked me to leave, saying that she was having an amazing dream.

I quickly left. With some disappointment. Shortly, the friend came forth from the room with a dream to share. Described to me was the exact experience I had just had outdoors. The same beatific chant singing from the sky. We were both elated and stunned by the beauty of the song from in the sky.

The Teachings

1) When we are open and receptive to the realization that "anything is possible," we remove not only our blinders, but the ear plugs.

2) When we are open and very yin, we discover that there is another world of rarified beauty.

3) Although I have no scientific knowledge of how this works, I have the personal experience of this realm of inner plane music that resounds in the airwaves. It is as real as hearing a dog

bark. So we are all invited to allow this feminine principle of receptiveness to be in full expression in our lives.

4) This teaching is profound, as it reminds us not to be stuck in our beliefs about reality.

Realm of Cosmic Consciousness: I Am Awareness (1981)

I have already said a little about this inner revelation in this book. I am including more here.

The Experience

In 1981, I had a nine hour experience/realization of Cosmic Consciousness. It was beyond teachers, teachings, traditions, religions, and paths. It was not a near-death experience. I was meditating.

I began meditating about nine p.m. one evening. I was sitting in a chair. The experience ended at six the next morning.

The entire experience that turned into realization was not anticipated. I did not even know it was possible.

The experience began the unveiling of the so-called mystery of consciousness. The experience did not reveal in scientific terms, but as Pure Awareness. Most of the experience, as it moved into realization, was and is beyond words.

I will share at the end my inspiration for finally sharing more of this.

Soon after I sat down, I began to meditate. I heard a dog barking outside. I heard this with my external ears. Then I became aware of the barking inside of me. There was no separation. The world was within. It was an amazing realization. The removed boundary of inside/outside changed my entire experience.

Next, I heard a car driving past. The same thing repeated itself. I could hear the car with my ears. Then I could hear it within my being. It seemed incredulous.

This experience continued to expand. I saw the town of Mount Shasta outside of me in my mind's eye and then inside of me. It continued to expand. Next the state of California was outside of me and simultaneously also within. Then the nation. And finally the entire Earth.

I felt no resistance to this expansion and depth of consciousness. I continued to open.

All of this time, I was fully aware of being Mary, sitting in a chair, meditating.

As my consciousness grew, I began to experience it as a higher Consciousness. Out in the expanded Silence and Vastness, I simply was no longer a seemingly personal I. I realized the Impersonal I as pure awareness. There was no thinking. There was no duality. There was only what I had read about, the splendor of the Isness. What Is. Desire and resistance and duality do not exist in this state of consciousness.

This Oneness Consciousness is everyone, everything, and everyplace. It does not feel odd or strange or unusual. It is simply What Is.

The only words I was aware of during this entire time came toward the end of the nine hours. And I did not hear actual words. It was a deep resounding knowing. A knowing outside of Time. The awareness was of I AM Awareness.

During this part of the experience after I had expanded past the

Earth, I began to fade from the "Mary meditating awareness." I realized, I Am Awareness, as the One that we are. Already Are.

There was no sentiment or attachment to the seemingly personal Mary. The Impersonal I was the All.

At six a.m., when I opened my eyes while still sitting in the chair, I could fully remember the experience.

I quickly felt this immense gap between my consciousness in my life as a mother of two daughters and what had just been realized. I felt this immense chasm. It was shocking to my mind and body.

I immediately began to ask, "How will I close this chasm? How may what I experienced be a part of my life? How may we live the mystical as practical?" I was overwhelmed with questions of closing that seeming gap.

Closing that chasm was the answer to a Seamless Life. It was the answer to living life at this level of Pure Consciousness.

The Teachings

Endless conscious books have been written on this subject. I will simply share a little of what I learned.

1) I Am Awareness is Pure Consciousness. Divine Mind. When we are open and free of the belief in separation, we are open to this realization.

2) In this state of consciousness, there is no fear and all of its offsprings, such as doubt, limitation. Non-duality is not even a concept to consider.

3) This state of consciousness is Oneness experienced, realized. And then we may allow it and it lives through us and AS us. And individuality is more fully in expression.

4) Everyone, everything, and everyplace is the I AM. I was given to know directly that "I Am is the only Presence Here." It is not an affirmation. It is not personal. It is not something to study. It is a living Christ Awareness. It is the Impersonal I. The One.

5) The world is inside of us. It is consciousness. I learned, that in demonstrating the Christ Presence, that the human consciousness full of beliefs in separation, thoughts, and conditionings begins to give way to Impersonal consciousness. Divine Mind reveals Itself. And Divine impulses and thoughts.

6) As we begin to practice this Christ Presence, we begin to trust it. Wonders begin.

Journey-HE...from the Stars unto the Stones

The Blue Kachina Realm:
A Visitation from Realm of Purity (1987)

Three Initiation Experiences

The Blue Kachina Realm Initiation came after three preparatory experiences. They were fully unexpected. They began June 1987.

I had been teaching sacred Soul Sounds and Soul Sessions in Sedona, Arizona. After the work in Sedona, I received a phone call requesting a Soul Session at Pyramid Lake, outside of Reno, Nevada. I said yes and began the journey to what I was told by a friend were ancient ceremonial grounds. I had my sleeping bag and after the session, I spent the night.

What a shock to awaken in the early morning to find that I was in "the home" of a bull, a cow, and a calf. They were near me. I am from Iowa and know how protective and dangerous bulls can be. Fear started to arise. I immediately realized that I could not stay in that fear. For some reason, as I went to the center of my being, I associated the word cow to moo and then to MU. And I had the thought that this was a "holy cow family" grazing near me. I realized I could drop the association with charging bulls. I calmly began to meditate on the living Christ, the light of presence. Very soon, my inner vision spontaneously opened.

First Experience

I was in an ancient world. I could feel the magic of that realm. It was a profound calm. One at a time, coming from the right side, was a procession. One at a time the native chieftains did come…in full regalia. I was a witness and I could deeply feel the sacred event. Sometime later, I was told that this type of clothing was their war clothing. I can only share the experience, as it unfolded. One at a time, these elder chiefs would walk in front of me, face me, and then bow down. I did not count how many there were, but there were many. Although none of them spoke any words to me, I was uplifted into a state of consciousness where I was "given to know" why this was happening.

I will do my best to describe their fully unexpected Visitation. These native elders understand the universal law of balance in all of Nature. They fully understand that a great change must happen and is happening in regard to this inviolate law of balance in all of Nature. Part of their role in the invisible inner planes is to hold sacred space for the arising of the divine feminine at this time. It will allow balanced and equal roles of man and woman. They fully realize the meaning and the necessity of the yin and yang balance. Man-woman balance. The masculine and feminine principle at play.

They understand that without that the world will create out-of-balance civilizations. And will continue to rise and to fall. And fail.

Homes, towns, states, and nations. All will be out of balance. This balance must start with within and extend out into man and woman. Woman must arise and give her gifts.

So why were these men bowing in front of me? They were not bowing to me. They were simply acknowledging one of my roles on Planet Earth which is to hold sacred space for the Arising of the Divine Feminine. And to hold space for equal man-woman roles. They seemed to fully know of my inner world of holding sacred space for what I call The Sacred Two. (See my book by that title.) I also call them Partners in Purpose, a term I learned via the teachings of Walter and Lao Russell.

These elder native chieftains are sacred space holders on the higher planes of existence for yin/yang balance.

The Teachings

1) There are very evolved beings of light that live in higher and invisible realms; they are with us in our activities here on the Earth.

2) We will continue to evolve and will not need words. Simply direct knowing. That was how this teaching happened.

3) There are beings of light that are fully dedicated to the universal Law of Balance and to the understanding of the masculine and feminine principles being in balance.

Second Experience

I was returning to my Mount Shasta home after this experience, but once I began the drive, I was unexpectedly and inexplicably guided to Mount Whitney. I had no understanding why. Yet.

As I arrived at the entry area, I found myself driving down a long road with tall rocks. They seemed to set the energy of entry. I felt as if I were entering another world. It was very other-worldly.

Once I arrived in a parking area, near the base of the mountain, I had a feeling to drive to where I was facing the mountain. I did not even feel as if I needed to leave my car. Again, there was a feeling that I must meditate on the Christ Presence. As I sat in this blessed presence, my inner vision again opened.

Before me was the Mayan Calendar. All my attention was on the central head with mouth open…tongue out. Formidable. Living. I was to enter. Fear came. Again…the awareness to enter and to stay focused on the Christ, the Light of Being. I entered.

In the inner vision, I was again a witness. I saw a mountain with a rock bluff that went straight up. It was very high. About two-thirds of the way up was a pathway for a sacred processional.

A procession of the balanced men and women through the ages.

Again, beginning from the right side, they began to walk. The HE and SHE of Creation. They were illumined and of such majestic divine power. Kings, queens. Princes, princesses. Shamans, shamanesses. Priests, priestesses. Seers and seeresses. That walked silently by. Two by two. They looked only straight ahead. They were dressed ceremoniously, as were the Native Chieftains. They were of such light and beatific beauty that it was difficult for me to stay conscious.

It was profound to behold and to take in.

They were clearly The Sacred Twos that have been holding sacred space for the universal principle of yin-yang balance down through the ages. They were man-woman Archetypes of such splendor. There was no sense of scholarly information. Just the sheer majesty and nobility of their roles.

The Teachings

1) There are Sacred Two Archetypes on the inner planes that are holding the balance for our plane of existence. Yet it is clear that we must live it on this plane.

2) There is a living principle, a law of balance, that humanity must align with and live.

3) There is a beauty beyond what the human mind may even conceive or imagine.

I returned to my home in Mount Shasta. It was still June, just a couple months before the well-known Harmonic Convergence.

Third Experience

A short time after my return home, another unusual experience came upon me. There seemed to be no preparation for this one either.

I awoke one morning and I was on my stomach. I mention this because I never sleep on my stomach. My arms were flapping, strangely, like wings. My body slightly lifted and an energy flipped me on my back. It happened too fast to know how to describe the energy. It simply happened very fast.

The light from the Realms of Light began to pour into my crown. Simultaneously the light from our precious Earth began to pour into my feet. The Sky energy descended. The Earth energy ascended. The two divine energies met in my heart center. The marriage of "as above, so below." It was an unutterable experience. Divine Love. Unconditioned. Transcendent. Beyond words.

I just lay in my bed for a long time in this luminous state of Being. It was an embodied experience and it was felt on a fully cellular level as well as in Consciousness. It was not an out-of-body experience. Again…yin/yang balance…

The Teachings

1) Stay attuned always. We never know when the Unutterable will lift us to an even more rarified frequency.

2) Be deeply in the current of life, so that when these exalted moments arrive, we are fully present.

The Blue Kachina Initiation

After some time of lying on my bed and just Being in the elevated resonance of the Infinite, my inner vision opened yet again. This time I was in the Realm of the Blue Kachinas. While I was witness to this, it all seemed so natural.

The Realm of the Blue Kachinas was revealed to me as a realm of purity. It is a realm of purity beyond the human mind. The human mind cannot conceive of this. Words…there are none.

I saw the Blue Kachinas. There were ten of them. They were standing in a circle, facing inward. They are electric blue white light of great luminosity. They are all female. They did not move. No details could be seen, including their faces. Simply a sense of emanating divine presence.

I have no memory of how long this lasted. It had and has a deep influence on my soul. There was a feeling of a calling. But to what?

I actually was guided to make two journeys to the Land of the Hopi. I wanted to get their interpretation of the meaning of the visitation. I also wanted to look through their art kachina books to see if I could find these Blue Kachinas which I experienced. I never did find those Kachina images that matched my experience.

My first trip out to Hopi Land I found no one to speak to. On the second journey out, a young Hopi man took me to see Grandmother Carolyn, the oldest female Hopi elder. I knocked on her door; she invited me in.

Grandmother Carolyn shared with me that the Hopi people were going through a difficult time. She explained to me that the Hopis were a divided people. She said they were addicted to alcohol and drugs and had turned away from their spiritual teachings. I was told that the Kachinas were no longer coming (at that time) to their ceremonies and that the ceremonies were empty. They were husks.

Grandmother Carolyn told me that now the Kachinas come to those of purity. Those with pure intent. Ones that are dedicated to Spirit. She told me that it was a great gift and a responsibility to be uplifted into that realm. Grandmother Carolyn told me that it would be up to me to open to the understanding of their communication, why there were ten and why they were all female.

As the years have passed, I see more and more the vital and even dire and urgent need for the feminine principle to be expressed on this planet. In all avenues of life! I see the need for the feminine perspective and gifts that are needed for humanity to live in balance. It is an urgent need.

Without the balanced expression of the yin and the yang of creation, we are lost. That balance allows the activation of the very natural activity of Oneness lived. And although we may list and delineate all of those aspects, we must know that they cannot be separated and dealt with as pieces. They are interrelated and interconnected. In the educational field, it is called inter-disciplinary. They all affect and influence one another. For instance, our social beliefs may influence art. Yet art may also influence social beliefs.

The Teachings

1) We may experience the direct knowing of a state of consciousness of purity that is beyond the mind's reach.

2) In that awareness of purity beyond the human mind, all that is unlike it falls away, as if it never were. Pure illusion.

3) It is possible to have purity of life. Purity of mind, body, emotions, lifestyle, and environment.

4) Belief in separation creates the obstacles to the awareness of this level of consciousness.

5) There is no compromise to the choices on this planet. We must begin to make the choice. Purity or Pollution. Each choice is a choice of one of those directions.

Purity is the measure. Purity is the gauge. Purity is the filter through which we create, produce, support, and use.

It may continue with the individuals that are pioneers of purity. But sooner or later it must be a collective choice.

To exist in harmony with the Earth we must learn to be one with the Earth.

6) This state of higher Consciousness is a state of exaltation. I do not refer to a "peak" experience. I refer to an ever present state of elevated consciousness. Pure Awareness. It is awaiting us. It ever Is.

And I would add that every day is an opportunity for all of us to deepen in this Pure Awareness, beyond the door of duality's drama.

Changing Woman Realm: Visitations (1980s)

These journeys, in meditation, continued to reveal to me that we ARE the "living revelations." There is nothing peculiar, strange, or unusual about this.

Often these realms are called archetypal realms. Many people study these archetypes in a scholarly manner. The study may greatly widen one's horizons. And they may help one walk through certain life's challenges as a hero or a heroine by providing a model.

And sometimes our inner vision may open and we behold an original archetype on the inner planes. It is a compelling experience. It is not a mental study. It is an awareness. And it may be felt.

The Experience

I did not know of the original archetypal realm of changing woman. In meditation, my inner vision would open. Numerous times I experienced Changing Woman. While it could be described as shamanic, it was also glowing with a galactic and heaven-world feel to it. It revealed a mastery.

I entered into a world, in Consciousness, of what could be called a liquid flow of life. A river. It is streaming, moving, luminous energy that is always shapeshifting. The actual morphing from form to formless to form is an experience of awe. It is a constant "letting go." Dying to form.

The beauty of the creations are inexpressible. Letting go becomes the art.

Here, the Changeless One (God) brings the change. It is fluid, flowing, and immediate.

I will share a short description of one of the many experiences in the Changing Woman Realm. I have much art that depicts this realm. It voices the experience better than words. Even the "poetic odysseys" in SHE…it is…who Remembers earlier in the book gives a feeling for Changing Woman. She is a magnificent archetype.

My inner vision opens. All is illumined, glowing. I see a woman of great beauty. She stands alone near the sea. She puts her foot into the sea. Immediately she begins to dematerialize as woman and in a few moments…she is the sea. And then she materializes back to woman. The woman leans over to touch the sweetest flower at the sea's edge. Slowly she shape shifts into a flower. And back to woman. This goes on, revealing many shifts into the natural world. Each merging…beautiful. Like a sacred enactment.

My description is like a "child's beholding." I did open and allow the ecstatic experience. I opened because it seemed to be offered from the Infinite as a gift. I saw that what we experience in Consciousness can be felt in our body. Embodied essence.

The Teachings

1) The archetypal realms are Impersonal and available to all to learn from.

2) There are archetypes in traditions around the world. There are also original archetypes that are not linked with a tradition. This is what I experienced.

3) The Changing Woman Realm is a powerful teacher of surrendering. Dying to the world of form.

4) The Changing Woman Realm is a powerful teacher of the Hopi teaching to us all…to jump into the River of Life. Flow. Don't hang on to the shore or even to a log or branches. Open to the Infinite.

Spider Woman Realm: Visitation (late 1980s)

I was not familiar with the traditional native archetypes. I was meditating on the Christ and my inner vision opened. I was in the Spider Woman Realm.

The Experience

This realm felt natural, flowing, and filled with what seems to be the magic of the Essence-world. All was luminous.

Spider Woman was revealed as Everywoman. It may seem impossible, but it all felt very real. She filled the sky. Her legs were made up of all women everywhere. Each woman was unique, different, welcomed. Each woman was dancing the Dance of the One. Spider Woman represented the One. Like The Great Mother.

In the realm, my eyes could zoom in or out. When I zoomed in, I could see women that I know and many I have not met. It was all the women of the world.

Each of their dances somehow kept the shape of Spider Woman's legs. There was an incomprehensible attunement. And yet the women were totally individual and self-governed.

I could feel the awe of witnessing this level of potential in the substance world of creation.

The Teachings

1) One of the main teachings here is the indescribable harmony that is experienced when ones align with the One. This is such a living example of that potential for humanity as the "one living organism that we are" is experienced both as Consciousness and as a body. No conflicts, no opposition, no war…

2) This dimensional archetype also revealed the beauty of each individual dance around the world.

3) This teaching exemplifies the power of movement and dance. And woman carries much inspiration for this cultural form of the Formless.

4) This teaching also denotes the importance of equal expression upon this Earth. This equal expression is important to the entire emerging culture, in all forms of Life expressing.

SHE...of the Circle

White Buffalo Calf Woman Realm: Visitation

After the sounds came through the birthing experience in 1975, which I described earlier, I began what I came to call Soul Sounds in the form of Soul Chants, Soul Drones, Soul Songs, and Soul Sounds. I began to do them every day. It was/is a powerful way to center if one attunes to the light of the heart (sometimes in other chakras) and then allows sacred sounds to emerge.

I began to feel them as Soul Sounds of World Birth. It was no longer personal. They held space for a larger birth that more and more people are aware of through direct experience and pure awareness.

The Experience

On this particular day, I was with a friend. I was making a Soul Droning sound. My friend went into some very beautiful and unusual sounds. I could feel another reality nearby. I asked her to continue with the same sounds. She did. She repeated them over and over. My inner vision opened. I was uplifted into the Realm of White Buffalo Calf Woman. She had an etheric presence. She enacted a ceremonial dance that was about The Sacred Two, the Partners in Purpose. Divine Purpose.

Years later, I found out that one of the gifts that White Buffalo Calf Woman carried in the traditional story was The Marriage Ceremony. This was indeed an astonishing dance.

I began to call this experience An Invitation into the Ancient Yin-Yang Circle. For that is indeed what the dance was/is about.

I have led many individuals through this initiation over the years. The experiences have all been fully unique and powerful.

It would be almost impossible to write about these initiations, since each person has fully different experiences and potent revelations. Each is benefitted in a totally different way.

This is a sacred ceremony, reserved for those who have aligned with Source and who are open to their true love partner. The outer yin-yang relationship. It is not a prescribed ritual. It unfolds spontaneously through the soul of the person being guided.

Their experiences have proved to shift both their beliefs and their lives. And it has all come from the wisdom that they do carry. It demands opening to the unconditioned Love.

The Teachings

1) White Buffalo Calf Woman's teaching is simple, yet power filled. It demonstrates an inexorable law. It is the law of balance. The law of love lived. It points to a foundation of all of life. The equal and balanced Dance of the One. It is the law of balance performed by all of Nature. It is in its utter simplicity the Law of Love.

The masculine and feminine principles in the world are opposite, but not in opposition. They complement. They are the fulfillment of Nature's natural order. Evaporate, precipitate. Contraction, expansion. Hot, cold. The examples are many in Nature's dance. Man and woman. Together they must live this higher law.

2) This teaching demonstrates how when there is the action of the yin principle, it must be balanced with the yang or an imbalance ensues. We may read history to see the imbalances in

our treatment of each other and the mistreatment of the Earth. The teachings simply point us to where changes are needed. They are needed in the home and all the way to national and international decisions and actions. There is a collective choice to be made, to avoid dire consequences.

3) White Buffalo Calf woman taught of the heightened power and awareness that may follow the uniting of Partners in Purpose. Sacred Purpose. I witnessed the joining of the energies. Words…none have I.

4) This potent and compelling archetype teaches and illustrates depth of true love, true union. It is romance so beyond the superficial levels that we see in movies and books of modern society. Those are as a shell or a husk of this deeper alignment that is possible.

5) This archetype reveals the sacred marriage. It is holy. Ones who have deeply attuned may open to this.

6) This archetype, when explored, allows one to traverse and navigate to realms beyond ordinary human beliefs and imaginings. It is transcendent. It is unique for each man and woman. It is as a key that opens doors.

The Beatific Realm (1980s and later)

This realm is a challenge to write about. I have not written of it before. I have kept it quite safe-guarded, as I was concerned that it would be fully misunderstood. It was/is a gift.

Occasionally I have slipped it into a Soul Session or a workshop if it served to awaken or educate by providing an example of how we create or miscreate in consciousness.

Everything happens via consciousness. We must be the guardian at the door of consciousness. As we stay in presence, no matter the situation we are presented with, we may open to higher frequencies.

The single example that I will give below will illustrate.

I did not see any of these "teachings" coming to me. They arrived unannounced. Like strangers. Arriving at one's door.

They are teachings, yes, but the teaching is given through experience. One may call it an initiation if it is new. They set a precedent. They also teach one how to handle life's challenges, no matter how seemingly horrific. They are practical. The mystical AS the practical.

As you read the description below, allow yourself to understand that all may ground this expansive knowing into one's seemingly personal and human life. In that way, shift of consciousness may come.

The Experience

It was in the late eighties. I was doing much painting and sculpting and spiritual studies, contemplations, and meditations. My daughters were sculpting their own lives. All was unfolding perfectly.

I loved to get still and go into the great Stillness. I would feel the calm of my own Being and that of the universe. One Breath. Holy Breath.

This day, I sat down to meditate. I was meditating on the Light of Presence. The Christ. As sometimes happened when I was meditating, my inner vision opened. My forehead seems as a screen for revelation.

This time I was shocked. I could see into the Hell Realm. I had not called for this. I had not opened to this. I felt fear begin to arise. I opened my eyes. I decided to try again. I closed my eyes. There it was again. The Hell Realm. I reopened my eyes. I don't recall how many times I repeated this. This realm did not go away.

I finally did an inner inquiry. I asked within what I was being shown and what was I being called to do.

I knew immediately. I was to do what I was shown to do when I was called to enter the mouth at the center of the Mayan Calendar. (I shared this earlier in the teachings.) I was asked to stay at One with the Christ and enter into this Hell Realm. Knowing that it was "illusory" did not help to alleviate the fear.

When I even slightly empathed the energies of this realm, I realized that this was a realm of "forgetfulness." Here, one could not remember the One. Here, one was what is often referred to as a lost soul.

I was frightened that if I lost contact with the One, I would not be able to listen to my higher consciousness.

It seemed to me that I was to receive yet another teaching by entering this realm, armed as a Being of Light. I entered.

As I entered I was utterly shocked. The hellish realm all around me began changing immediately. It began to reconfigure. It was luminous. The beauty was beyond the mind's imaginings. It began to spread out from me. Beatific! That is the only word I can find. Rapturous beauty. The illusion of the hell realm was simply a human creation of the mind. The hellish configuration was amassed through the ages. Much of humanity rests in these beliefs. They feed this realm.

We are in another time.

We are the living revelations.

Those revelations birth within our heart.

They bring change.

Change…through our choices and how we live.

The Teachings

1) This teaching/initiation from this exalted realm, an unseen realm, is quite straightforward.

We are all being shown "how" to stay in our True Identity, as

Light, as Presence. We are to identify with our body of light. And let it emanate. And see it everywhere. Now.

Then the Energy will re-configure and revealed is the illumined realm of the holy.

2) We do not need to have a near-death experience or an actual death experience to experience this realm of the holy.

3) Collectively and individually, we need to discern what our beliefs and opinions are and let them go. Ask, within, to be shown the truth.

4) We may open to Beauty, the Essence of Life, beyond all imaginings and concepts.

5) We may see that this astral realm of human thoughts is fluid, moving, changing. It is impermanent. Its nature is fleeting.

Thought waves moving and constantly changing.

6) Attune to the Unmanifest. And see the illusory nature of manifest life.

EarthCare Global TV: A Vision and Impartation (1996 and 1997)

I had been feeling something wanting to birth from within for months before this vision came. It came to me in two stages. The first came in 1996.

The Experience

During the night, I awoke and in inner vision I saw a light ray come down toward me. Somehow I could read the message it carried. Or a better way to say it is, "I was given to know." It carried the message of The People's Network. TPN. I began researching and contacting people everywhere, but did not find what had streamed to me.

The second stage came in 1997. I spent quite a few weeks in retreat for I still felt something coming from within. This second time I was given an awareness for EarthCare Global TV. (One may now visit the website by that name.)

I was guided to go to Crestone, Colorado to retreat for the winter. I was to have all the information that had come to me typed. I did that. It was years later before I realized that it was for Internet TV. Several people had tried to inform me of that, but it took a while for me to actually realize that.

The Teachings

1) We all may open to the Intelligence of the Universe.

2) We must open to receive our exceptional and unique and needed part in this expanding Universe.

3) What we may be guided to do next may "drop into consciousness" with no thinking. It does not need to be a laborious mental process.

4) The Intelligence of the Infinite is always guiding. We must be open, connected, listening. At One.

The Animal Soul Realm: Visitations and Messages (1996 and on)

First Experience

Here is what began to happen. As I meditated on the Light of Presence, my inner vision would sometimes open and I would be uplifted into the animal realm. It is luminous. Loving. Powerful. Christed. I call it the Soul Realm of the Animals. The animals began to appear before me. Sometimes alone. Sometimes there were many. They would look at me.

At times they would appear and communicate. In one instance, my daughter's deceased cat, that I was very close to, came to me. As she stood before me in this realm, she turned to walk into the forest. As she did, she began to shape-shift. She did shape-shift into the Tribe of Cat. She appeared as many types of wild cats.

The Teachings

1) I could understand the messages with no words. One message was/is that cats want to have their feet on the Earth.

2) The cats also conveyed the message that they want to spend much time out of doors.

3) It was very clear that they wanted to be respected for their independent nature.

Second Experience

Another experience in the Soul Realm of the Animals was the

appearance of many animals. One after another animal would appear until finally there were large numbers appearing from the jungle. I could see their soul depth through their beautiful and penetrating eyes.

The Teachings

1) The animals let me "wordlessly know" that animals have rights.

2) The animals informed me that they are needing humans as the Voice of Animals to bring changes regarding care, protection, and co-existence.

3) The animals let me know that they need their habitats. They and their environment play an important role in the very web of life. It became clear to me that humans must awaken to the devastation of their environment, the home of the animals. And a place of refuge for humans!

4) The animals made it very clear to me that they do not want to be caged.

5) The animals revealed to me that they can communicate much to us, if we would but listen.

During and even after these journeys into the animal realm, I began receiving messages from them in the form of poetry and paintings. I recorded these messages and they became a recording called *Return to Oneness*.

I realize that we all may be the voice of animals.

(As a child, I had already communicated with crabs on the beach, dogs, and squirrels.)

This experience took that communication to another level.

6) All who are drawn to be animal communicators may do that. There must be the pure intention to co-exist with the animal realm. We must respect them and their habitats. And we must realize that we are not more important than they. We must realize animal rights.

The Overlighting: Visitation and Healing (on trip to Brazil)

As I was writing the experience about the Animal Realm, I had a strong impulse to include the "Overlighting" experience. Although I have had many overlighting experiences, this one stands out as important to share. It has some potent teachings.

The Experience

Out of the blue, when I neared fifty years, I began to experience full body nausea. I went to doctors and they could find nothing. I went to endless alternative doctors and healers for thirteen years. I even sold my two houses to have the finances to go to these practitioners. I spent the equity of both homes trying to get well. All meant well, but there were no results or changes.

One day I was in the Santa Cruz mountains to do an art exhibit at an event. I went into a tiny restaurant to eat and picked up a local paper about conscious events. I read an article about John of God, a healing medium, who lives in Brazil. I could feel energy rush through my entire body as I was reading. All my cells felt lighted. I was to go to Brazil and see this man.

I had become so sick from this nausea that I knew I had to be guided. Now.

I returned home, did an "art sale," my first ever, on the phone. I earned enough to go to Abadiana, Brazil, to be with John of God.

As I was flying to Brazil, I found myself falling into an utter surrender. I had nothing. No marriage. Children grown and gone. Both homes now sold and gone. Money gone. Health gone.

And yet, Grace was flowing.

Dear friends, who take groups to John of God, helped me make all the arrangements to go to Brazil. That included a lovely family in Brazilia, where I landed, who hosted me on the way down and the way back. That included also arranging rides for me to and from Abadiana. They picked me up at the airport, provided a room and meals, and gave me a tour of their city. Beautiful people.

While on the plane, flying to Brazil, I prayed for either full recovery or to leave this plane of existence. I do not believe we need to be in sickness. I remember also saying, "If I am not going in the right direction in my life, please reveal that to me and I will change." I was then shown.

My prayers led to being deep in the presence of the Divine. And that led to a deep silence and peace that was simply acceptance of the moment.

At that moment, I felt an immense and divine overlighting. It seemed above me, but I could also feel it in my body. It was a deep cellular illumination. It both enveloped me and filled my being. It was grace.

My eyes were closed. My inner vision opened. I was aware that the overlighting was Mother Mary. In silence, she showed me a single page from her Book of Life. What was seen on the page was alive and moving. It was like watching a movie. Mother Mary was putting her hands and arms into the auric field of ones who were sick. They were then Whole. A healing had happened.

It was immediate. She then showed me a single page from my Book of Life. It was a shock. I was doing the same thing with my hands and arms as I had just seen her doing.

With no words, I communicated to Mother Mary that I did not know how to do that. She wordlessly let me know that the response was to be "yes." For I was the one who had requested to be shown if there was yet another expression of my life that I was to know about.

I said "yes." I was clear, in that moment, that I would be guided.

And, in the very next moment, I was Whole. The nausea was gone. It was completely gone. The overlighting was gone.

I even wondered if I needed to go to Brazil now. Mother Mary works through the medium, John of God, but she did not even wait for me to get down there.

I decided to remain there for the 2 1/2 weeks and do all of the meditations and visits to John of God. It was wonderful being there. I realized that through the focus that John of God holds at the Casa de Dom Inacio healings happen. All of it was the result of being One with the Light of Being and surrendering. And grace did come.

The Teachings

1) I learned the importance of full dedication to the Inner Presence. It allows full surrender. That IS full surrender.

2) I learned the power of deep surrender to What Is.

3) I learned that another one who is in service to Love may

be the needed "two or more to gather together" to heighten the consciousness to Divine Consciousness. To the frequency of Wholeness. It is a state of consciousness and is beyond human concepts of human wellness and sickness. It is the divine Wholeness that Already IS.

4) I learned that time is not necessarily needed to experience Wholeness.

5) I learned that these Beings of Light are there to help us to "help ourselves."

6) I learned that my litany of losses were not losses. They were simply a way to have a new canvas of Life.

7) I experienced a gain. An increase in divine Awareness. An experience of that Unspeakable Energy alighting. It is priceless.

The Realm of Illumination: Perfection Manifest (2013)

All of these experiences in higher frequencies and realms have come unexpectedly. They simply showed up as Life in such a natural way. As we stay attuned to and identified with the Field of Light, it is our True Life that shows up. If we are in duality and in negative beliefs and reactions, then those things show up as our imbalanced human life. It is a choice.

The Experience

The weather was beautiful. A friend and I decided to make a half hour hike to a pristine waterfall. It was a relaxing walk. Peace everywhere. When we arrived, I suggested that we each take time to go off and be silent and then get together to eat and talk. After we had eaten, my friend spoke of a pain in her shoulder. I said I would do a Wholeness meditation. We closed our eyes and I led the meditation. I said to my friend that all that was necessary for her was to do the holy breath. That is, consciously breathe and be one with the light, open and receptive.

After a short time, I felt the higher Energies of joy on a cellular level. I asked my friend if she felt them also. She did. I said let us just bathe in this field of light for a while longer.

Then, after some time, I opened my eyes.

I can only announce my response as a holy beholding.

Everything was illumined. Glowing. No longer did everything look like solid 3-D. The waterfall was illumined. The pool below was illumined. And the surrounding foliage. Even the rocks.

Beauty. Luminous Beauty.

Once I took it in, I asked my friend to open her eyes and tell me what she saw. She did. She saw and witnessed everything that I saw. No words describe our awe of this experience.

It reminded us of the special light effects in some movies, such as in Avatar. But this was not a screen on the wall.

I said that I would like to just take it in. We simply sat in silence.

It felt like viewing a coming attraction for humanity.

The Teachings

1) Stay open-minded so that the so-called impossible may be possible.

2) Stay open to witness the natural and supernatural as One. No separation.

3) Stay aware that the ordinary is the extraordinary.

4) Stay aware that we live in a quantum universe of light.

5) Be aware that vast changes are coming for humanity.

6) Be willing to let go of beliefs and false concepts.

The Leap off the Metaphoric Cliff (1971)

There have been numerous experiences that I did not intend to share in this book, but I found that as I wrote grew this compelling impulse to share them. Many people who know this next experience have asked me to write about it giving more detail. They told me that it gave them courage and trust. (I would say that courage and trust come from within, but I do believe that stories can catalyze in many ways.)

The story that I am going to share now happened just after the Soul Realm of Joy experience. That was the near-death experience via a car collision. I mentioned, that after that collision, that I could see the white light aura around living things.

At the time all of this happened, I was a college instructor, teaching English and Communications at a small Oregon College.

I had been shaken to my core in the near-death experience. I could not quit thinking of the awareness that I had at the moment of impact. It was a realm of joy and exalted feelings. I became aware that this higher joy was available all the time. I was also painfully aware that my current life seemed safe, secure and stable, but I was not in joy.

Now I had a measure for joy. I was nowhere close.

I was now strongly drawn to noticing this emanating light that I could now see. I continued to feel that I was to proceed in my life as an artist. (I had spent summers going to the University of Wisconsin in Fine Arts to get another degree.)

I could feel the growing inspiration to express as an artist! It was indwelling and strong.

The Experience

One day I simply "leapt off the metaphoric cliff." And I began to fly.

I quit my teaching position. I had very little savings. I told my now ex-husband that I needed him to be "mom" for six months. Although I did not want to leave my daughter, the ex demanded that I not take her with me.

I made my life transition. It was done.

This leap happened in 1971. At that time, there were only a small number of us making such radical shifts.

I bought a Kelty back pack and a sleeping bag. I filled the pack with one change of clothes, a coat, a hairbrush, a toothbrush and my loved art paper, Rapidograph pens, and magic markers. And passport and cash. I traded my Pontiac sedan in for a used Econoline van. Home.

I could not get India out of my mind. Probably because of the *Be Here Now* book and everyone then knew about the Beatles and their spiritual sojourns to India.

I asked college friends in Kentucky if I could leave my vehicle there when I flew overseas. They said yes. I flew into Madrid, Spain, hitchhiked to the border, and crossed to Morocco and into Marrakech. After falling in love with the bazaars and the international writers living for almost nothing on the roofs of buildings, I left for Italy. Then to Crete, where I had a dream of my Christed self as a baby and also felt one with the ancient culture there. The people were giving, loving. After Crete, I journeyed to Greece. In Athens, I spent some time just enjoying the people, the food, the produce markets of such beauty. I was loving the international travel. I was also attuning to where I would go next. People warned me not to go to India because of diseases. I was called.

I left on a private bus owned by a German man. The bus was full. I was traveling to New Delhi on a trip that was to take 17 days. It took 30. The bus continued to break down and opened many adventures as we made our way across Turkey, Afghanistan, Iran, and Pakistan to New Delhi.

Later I took a taxi to Kashmir where I lived on a boat on Dal Lake in Srinagar. I was learning to get quiet and find the indwelling presence. There was no problem getting up early to meditate. The lake was full of men in little boats in the early mornings, shouting "choc-o-late, choc-o-late."

I did small ink drawings everyplace that I traveled. I used Rapidographs for the drawings and then used the very bold magic markers. The drawings I did in a most intuitive way. I put the pen on the paper and did the entire drawing without lifting my hand. All the drawings seemed to be transcendent beings of light, walking from a faraway horizon. Some had a rudimentary landscape.

The drawings were my beginning of visionary art. The figures felt like Christed beings. I was so in love with drawing.

This art expression from a Soul level allowed me to feel some of what my life was about. I still had much confusion if I thought about what I would do for a living when back in America. But I did not let my mind stay there for long. It was too scary to look at.

I had purchased some beautiful small gold frames while in

Venice. I had them shipped back to the U.S. They would literally become the frames for my first three visionary art exhibits. One of those shows was exhibited at the college where I had previously been teaching.

After leaping off the cliff, I was now pioneering visionary art shows. It was now 1972. The art sold. I did not look back.

There have been many small and big challenges along this path of leaping off the cliff. Would I change it? No. It has been a perfect journey. It has allowed the soul's expression. Is jumping off the cliff for everyone? No. It must be guided from the Withinness.

Many around me at that time were aghast at my choices. At that time, I saw no other way. It seemed clear that what I did was a calling.

When I returned to Oregon and picked up my daughter, now two and one-half years, we set out traveling across the Southwest and West Coast. It was 1972 and I was hearing about spas and hot springs, healing and fasting centers, ashrams, communes, organic and bio-dynamic farms, health-food stores. Organic products. I was being introduced quickly to a culture that felt alive, free and dynamic. This is the world I would enter. And I would continue to draw.

My daughter and I traveled to farms, centers, and ashrams for one and one-half years. By that time I had an old pick-up with a camper on the back. That was our home.

I won't delve into the amazing discoveries that I made during those years, but I will mention a couple of the experiences. I was hired by One Life in Venice, California, before it had really even launched, so I witnessed the beginning of a health food store by three men with no money. They had vision and deep inspiration. I also helped a group that brought Muktananda to America for the second visit.

I was also praying deeply for a place to land. To live. My daughter was soon going to be entering kindergarten. I prayed to know where we should live and put down roots. I wanted that. I prayed for a place that would be perfect for she and I and a place that would be conducive to spiritual growth.

Soon after that, I had a dream and I was shown a location that was home. On my next I-5 trip in California, I stopped in Mount Shasta. I saw the spot at Stewart Mineral Springs that was shown in the dream of "home." We moved to Mount Shasta.

The Teachings

1) When we jump off the cliff, we are giving ourselves to the Infinite. We are in flight with the beloved. A soul flight. Our inner navigation guides and directs.

2) We must open immediately to intuition, insights, and guidance.

3) We must trust and take action.

4) We must be ready for change. The Changeless One brings the change.

5) We must leave all blaming behind.

6) We must stay identified as the Infinite Presence. Embodied Presence.

7) We must embrace our own unique spiritual journey.

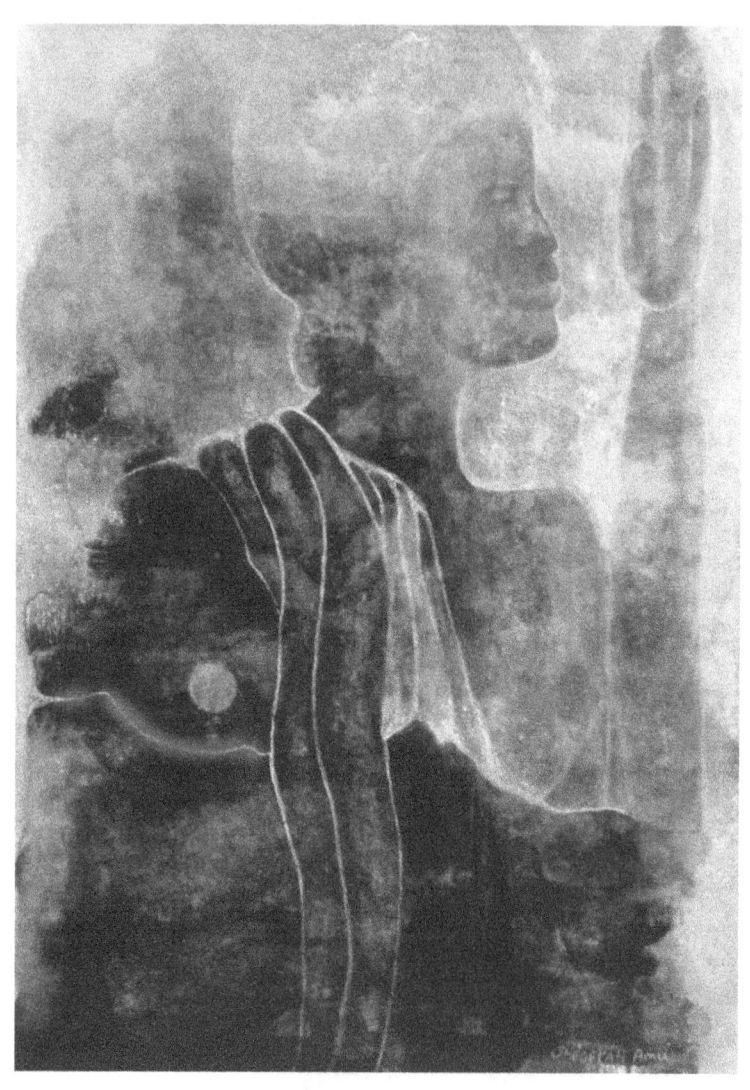

Greetings from the Stars

The Great Mother: An Embodiment (2016)

Within the heart dwells a realm of consciousness that predates history. It is a living link to our origins and beyond.

There may be moments in our lives when we so retire from the seeming external world that we enter the Timelessness. The place that is not a place, state, realm. Just Silence.

This is a departure from the world of society. Instead we enter the "darkness" described by Marija Gimbutus in *The Language of the Goddess*. It is as a black womb understood by the ancient matriarchal cultures. Black was a symbol of the womb. It was considered life-giving. White was as a bone or death. Such a different system of thought. Circular.

In this disappearance into the "darkness" is the possibility of the reappearance of new life. That new life may take many forms. From the Unknown to the Known. The Great Mystery and then the unveiled Mysteries.

This shift of consciousness is available to all. Yet the shackles of society are often tight and pervasive. Some are not ready to venture into these realms, these divine regions. This beauty may open to us, educate us, and uplift us. And we do change.

When we enter the great Stillness, we may be given a gift. We do not attune to Source by seeking a gift. Or a realm. Or another dimension.

We enter by dying. Dying to what we regard as our external world, including thoughts and dreams. We simply open to be one with the Infinite. It is our unspoken call to allow the Unmanifest to manifest as our very Being. And to extend that awareness to everyone, everything, and every place. The One as the many!

I want to share an experience with/as The Great Mother. I was not trying to have an experience in a divine realm. I was simply going to the Source. Empty. Allowing. This was not an out-of-body experience. It was fully embodied. It was simultaneously experienced and realized.

It was beyond the function of the thinking mind, so to describe this wordless experience is delicate and gossamer.

The Experience

I have played the role of spiritual educator for large numbers over many decades. By the word educator, I mean holding sacred space for another person. Holding space for their Wholeness that Already Is, that who they are may birth. (I am making a distinction from the role of teacher that usually has a lot of information to share.)

I have held sacred space for many in what I call Sounds and Signings of the Soul. This practice creates a notable yin and receptive space for new expression to birth. Experience emerges from the mystical to the ordinary, the practical.

One is the living language of the Great Goddess.

The practice calls for being fully present in the Presence, that one allows the "present" which comes forth. One must be in a very refined attunement to the Inner Perfection and allow. Open and allow. Allow Silence. Sounds. Signings (movements) and/or Stillness.

In that space is created a very conducive environment. Revelation, awareness, experience may come with the exalted energy of the Primordial One. The Cosmic One. (This may come to anyone anytime as Grace.) Sometimes it comes simply by our opening.

The One is not a Being; rather, it is Beingness. Isness. And it is everywhere. We may call it I Am Awareness. Pure Awareness.

I was sharing the experience of Sounds and Signings of the Soul with one who came to me. I was Soul Sounding to the cosmic sound of Om, when my sounds became a soul chant. It became quite loud. Then it just stopped. I found myself simultaneously embodied consciously, as well as being one with The Great Mother archetype that was manifest from the Stillness.

My left arm began making a circling clockwise movement. Like holding a space for alchemy. It was clear it was a portal for energy from this holy realm. After a while, the circling arm stopped and the entire upper part of my body began making the clockwise circling movement. I continued to feel the exalted energies pouring in. And I was aware the energy was emanating from within me into the room.

This continued for quite some time. It was like being aware of Stillness, an archetypal realm and the physical realm all at the same time. It is a beatific expansion and it awaits humanity.

As this was happening, I simply quit consciously holding space for the other person, as I usually did. I was simply to allow this experience and realization.

The Teachings

1) Soul attunement and expression, such as Sounds and Signings of the Soul, serve as portals to other realms and dimensions.

And a portal into the Christ Presence of God. Stillness.

2) We may experience the expanded consciousness that is offered by original archetypes. We may do this while we are in the embodied experience of seeming time and space.

3) This experience may also open us to experience deeply the Silence. And realize one's true spiritual identity.

4) It is clear that these deep archetypal experiences that elevate one are there for all. Anyone may open to them.

5) Marija Gimbutus understood the language of the goddess. She understood as one who studied for decades the goddess cultures of the ancient matriarchal periods. She showed the depth of understanding of the cosmic force through the body.

This experience in Sounds and Signings of the Soul allows us to experience the divine feminine principle and be the living language of the goddess via sound, silence, signings, and stillness. I often call the movements or still postures soul glyphs or soul body mudras. We are postured by the Infinite and we allow. This is a great practice for the expression of Perfection which is our very life.

What was accessed in this session was a true and overlighting expression of SHE…the Mother of the World. She has been described with many names, in many cultures. The Mother. Mother God. The Great Goddess. And myriad Goddess names.

Afterword: I have practiced Sounds and Signings of the Soul since 1975. This practice may open many doors and portals. I have experienced the ones below and many others. They are available to all who open.

I will list a few gifts that may come:

Access inner hearing of music of the realms, music of angelic realms, and music of celestial realms.

Access inner vision and inner feeling.

Access an aspect of your soul's mission.

Access new realms, new forms, and Divine Imaginings.

Access the kingdoms of the Mother, the elements, and other dimensions.

Access tones and body configurations which open dimensional doors.

Open to Presence more deeply.

Open and allow free expression.

Open to the ability to Speak Up.

Open to know, beyond tradition's door.

Open to see beyond shadows, into the Light of knowing.

Open to experience the planetary initiation and passage into the "Once upon a Non-Time." The ever-present Timelessness.

Open to inspiration to create BEAUTY beyond the mind…and know how to manifest it.

Allow the cosmic sounds to emanate into the world through your body. A sound vessel.

Part four:
Afterwords

About the Title

Galactic Shamanism is the story of Balance. It is the story of finding the inner marriage of earth and sky, of the HE and SHE of all Creation. It is the polarities merged as the Divine Presence. From that place comes Ancient Remembering of the ONE. From that place in our consciousness can we enact the True Story…the Trustory. From that place, in the Silence, we can Know for ourselves.

About the Writing Style

As a past teacher of high school and college English, it would seem I might conform to established patterns of prose or poetry. However, the first part of this book came to me at pre-dawn and dawn, when I was not in an intellectual mode.

I was awakened by the Divine Presence and I recorded what easily came. As I sat ecstatically in the Silence, the words flowed forth with a clear rhythm and cadence and with certain tones, intonations, and pauses. I have recorded them exactly as they came.

The writing is more what the literary world would refer to as stream-of-consciousness. This free expression allows me to give easy birth to the feelings of the Presence as I write, that the feelings can more easily be felt by the reader.

The purpose of the writings is to catalyze Rememberings of Oneness and to inspire and evoke Rememberings of Life as Living Ceremony of the ONE.

I had only intended to share my spiritual experiences, my

expressions, and my reality through art, sculpture, sound, and dance. They are a rather safe guise for free expression, and one can be visionary and multi-dimensional without raising eyebrows. However, there is something about being direct with words.

When we actually voice an experience, such as "I remember before I was born," or "I remember the planet I am from," unless we are very discerning, it can create communication gaps that are difficult to bridge. You are in the visible world and you have just shared an immense piece from the invisible world. How is it going to be bridged? Up until now, I have mainly shared via universal and sacred art and in private Soul Sessions, when appropriate.

As the writings continued to pour forth, I realized that it was time to share more of my multi-dimensional reality with words as well. It was revealed to me that the writings are filled with "trigger phrases" that can assist others to Remember who they are and why they are here.

The writings serve to inspire Ancient Rememberings of the ONE, so that each person can add his or her own piece of The Story…The Divine Story. When one person shares a shard of the "Divine Template," others are activated.

We are all here Remembering together…and our pieces fit together. As the pieces come together and we see more and more of the Big Picture with our inner vision, our "aerial viewing" abilities, we will realize there is no puzzle! It is only the pieces of the Many, being revealed as the ONE!

About the Art

The mixed media paintings in this book are by Mary Saint-Marie; they are translations of her odysseys into the Archetypal Inner Realms of Light…in feeling, vision, and sound.

About the Sacred Two

There are many sacred couples with known Divine purpose now coming together. They are great gifts upon this planet…great inspirations for us all, for they embody inner and outer Balance in their lives. They are the HE and SHE of all Creation joined as the ONE.

Mary carries the *Gift of Ceremony* and has been given a ceremony to share by White Buffalo Woman and her Sacred Two in the Sacred Circle, which is available upon request. It is a Ceremony Initiation into The Sacred Two, entering the ancient Yin-Yang Circle. Mary draws on Divine Archetypes, such as White Buffalo Woman and Beauty-SHE of all the fairy tales.

Mary also has art available which reflects The Sacred Two.

About the Male Archetype

I am beginning to have glimpses on the inner planes and the outer planes of the Divine Masculine Archetype…it is majestic beyond words…and in full oneness with woman. The mystery… unfolds…it is glorious…

About Life as Living Ceremony

In the mid-eighties, in the middle of the night, I awoke and experienced the following:

Coming down from the ceiling, in luminous golden letters in a vertical line, were the words, Gift of Ceremony. I knew immediately what it meant, for I had been creating ceremony all my life. Life for me was more like temple tending. And I was now doing ceremony sessions with many individuals, helping them see the celebration of each moment of the Land of Now. With the glowing vertical column of those three words, Gift of Ceremony, I knew that the Presence of the ONE was conveying to me the message…that I carried the Gift of Ceremony and that I was to help reveal to others, who had not yet awakened to it, that they, too, carry the Gift of Ceremony. All carry the Gift of Ceremony. Not all remember.

I do not refer to Ceremony as a formal ritual from a tradition or otherwise. I refer to the new day that is dawning, for a new consciousness is dawning. It is the consciousness of Life as Ceremony, of Life as Living Ceremony, of Life as the spontaneous Living Ceremony of Spirit, each day, each moment of the NOW. Ceremony, in this sense, is a conscious celebration. Life as celebration! The forms we can use to celebrate it are infinite and can spring up in the moment as we allow. And finally, Life as Ceremony remembers that we are living in the Garden. We are already living in The Garden. That is Grace.

Since 1971, my life has been filled with spontaneous revelations and illuminations from Spirit. Many of these were an entering into the Divine Archetypal realms in meditation and seeing "the archetypal dance of the Many as the ONE," that was possible to enact upon this planet. I was in ecstasy, rapture, bliss, Oneness in ways that defy imagination or even description.

Constantly my questions were: How do I maintain and sustain such awesome states of consciousness? How do I live and share that which I have beheld? How can I give it form and expression?

The following image very simply shows why most of the planet is not in balanced bliss.

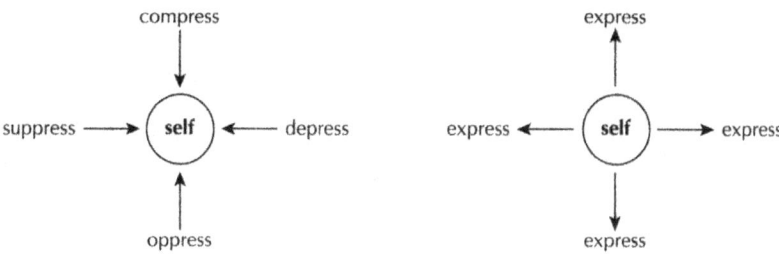

A person who lives from outside pressures and information is never connected to one's inner Self. That person is living from the outside in and is disconnected from his/her own direct Knowing. A person who gives expression to one's direct connection with Self, Source, Spirit, the Presence, God, etc. begins to find the joys of Life as a Living Ceremony. That person lives from the inside out in the fulfillment of one's true identity.

I had an immense illumination at the beginning of the nineties of how Life as Living Ceremony would ensue. It began thus. I felt to have twelve people gather on Mount Shasta at 3:30 a.m. on January 1, 1990 to meditate. Twelve of us gathered and meditated and I immediately had my inner vision open. This is what I saw. I was aware of being pure Consciousness viewing a scene from out in space. I could look down at the planet and see thousands of what I was given to call starships surrounding the planet. They appeared as glowing balls of light sending beams of light onto the planet. The feeling was full of Love. It was a peaceful scene. Then, in an instant, my consciousness was a zoom lens into the Yucatan and I was aware of the light beams streaming into an ancient stone stele in Palenque. Some steles have inscriptions, some have symbols, and some have faces. This one had a face.

As I watched the light touch the stone, I was aware that similar stone steles around the globe were simultaneously being touched by this light ray. I was aware that the stones carried ancient encodements and that the light was activating the encodements. When the stone was touched by the light, it became alive in a way that words cannot describe. The activation of the encodements was to begin a new phase of the enfoldment of Spirit on the planet, through willing ones.

The activated encodements are to begin the "dissolving of tradition" as we know it. Traditions have been and are a blessing, as "containers of Light and Truth." Throughout eons of darkness, we have needed these protections, these fortresses of Light provided by traditions. Now there is a growing legion of people who are ready to go directly to God, to the Presence. For them, tradition is dissolving. The activation of the ancient stone steles is a measure of support provided for those who no longer need an intercessor, a medium, an interpreter, a guide in their going to Source. The activation is an energy release that supports those who want to allow the living Presence of God to enact directly through them. So thus began the nineties.

When that direct living in the ONEness occurs, Balance will become a demonstrated quality. We have all noticed the growing passionate interest in Angels and Shamans. That passion has grown into the love of harps and drums, for good reason. The harps bring forth celestial music from the angelic realms and spheres; the drums and rattles bring forth the rhythms of the Earth Mother. Earth and Sky.

As this polarity dance of sky and earth continued, I began to ask, "Where are the Angels that land and the Shamans who fly? Can't we have harps and drums in the same song? How do earth and sky dance? Where is the balance and the interconnectedness? Truly, where is the divine intercourse? Where is the marriage? And how does this all relate to male/female alliance and Balance upon this Earth?"

As time went by, I realized among the ones who were wanting God, that there were those star beings, angels who needed a "landing pad"…to allow Spirit to descend into matter and there were those shamans, earthy beings who needed a "launching pad"…to allow an ascension of consciousness to experience other subtle realms and dimensions or just simply to feel the Presence.

As my parents were both professional pilots, both in and out of the Air Force, I learned the flying jargon early and began to realize that to have Balance on this plane of existence, that we must have both "ground school" and "flight school." This means we must be "in the world, but not of the world." For Balance, we must launch our consciousness to the "on High" and then we must "land" that which is ours (individually or in groups) to do, to say, to sing, to dance, to heal, to form, and on and on.

Let us begin this day to live Life as a spontaneous Ceremony of Spirit…ongoing, never ending, eternal. That bringing of earth and sky together in our lives is Balance…is Galactic Shamanism.

> *"Life as Living Ceremony is the honoring*
> *of Creation's Sacred Dance*
> *of the ONE come as the Many."*

About the Changes:
Prophecies are Messengers of Change

Prophecies are Messengers of Change. The years come and the years go. Many there are among you who rise above the day-to-day prattle of human life and who see far into the human future, the perennial handwriting on the wall. Because there are so very many imbalanced actions of miscreation, borne out of a sense of separation from ME…the Infinite ONE… these flights into the human future are often very grim, for they are based on actions presently lived. These flights are called prophesies…and they are nigh filled with warnings, messages of needed change…or comes…impending disaster, destruction and doom.

These prophetic messages are powerful and timely pre-warnings. Prophesies are "messengers of change." They are not harbingers of disaster, of Armageddons predicted and destined. They are fate only for those who look away, ignore and refuse to change.

For those who refuse to change, change comes anyway and blows across lives…sweetly…moving some as a willow tree and breaking unyielding ones, fraught with crystallizing seasons' past.

For those who change, when the warning doth "wave its flag," the flight of fiendish vision never comes. The prophecy for them does leave no tracks…ere their lives no longer foretell a future of good fortune gone astray.

Rather do the lives of untold persons become a Light unto the world. A Light that also is a flight into the future. This future is the ever searched for Garden that can never be reached by map. This future is the present lived in love, in Presence.

This is the only prophecy of Truth. It looks beyond the fields of miscreation and sees another world. A world of heaven-sent visions…thus heaven-sent prophecy. The choice is clearly to be made by each individual with free will choice as it is.

The most that each individual can do is to live the inner vision that they see. Each vision lived will complete a piece of the grander picture and cause others to see their part of the ONE vision. And one by one, then two by two, in ever increasing numbers will the vision of the ONE be fulfilled. No workshop, book or teacher can give one this. It is a solitary flight to the vision of the All.

About the Artist-Writer

Mary Saint-Marie is a visionary artist who paints sacred and mystic art with images that inspire and reflect Soul Remembering. Her art is born of inner odysseys into the "once upon a non-time." She sits at the edge of paradox and shares the union of visible and invisible, form and formless...the sacred mergings. She holds the space for the landing of the Divine Archetypal Realm Templates. She gathers images of the Eternal.

The ceremonial expression of Mary began in 1975 during the birth of her second daughter. This initiated the birth of Sounds and Signings of the Soul (soul sounds, movements, configurations, and body glyphs). She has also initiated many individuals and groups into the Divine Archetypal Feminine and The Sacred Twos.

This work expanded into Sacred Enactments of Ancient Remembering in the early 90s. These multi-media ceremonies are shared to inspire and catalyze "the multicultural and multidimensional blendings and bleed-throughs happening across the lands and across the seas unto these very times." They are shared to gather the Star-Stone Tribes, the Soul Tribes. They are offered to deeply touch the Presence of the One...as together...we enact World Birth.

Art of the Soul has been exhibited in over 150 individual and group exhibitions across American and in Europe in galleries, expositions, symposiums, retreats, and workshops. Mary's art has been featured on cards, books, calendars, and magazines, such as *Quest, Mystic Pop,* and *Anemone* in Japan. Mary has been featured on television nationwide via many stations, including the Wisdom Channel. Her art has been televised across Germany. The mystic art and work has been on and in many books, including *One Source Sacred Journeys, Songs from the Edge of Everything,* and *The Ways of Spirit.* In addition, her art may be seen on and in her other books. Mary has been pioneering art exhibitions that reveal universal principles of Oneness since 1972.

Mary has a BA in Education and English. She taught high school and college English for eight years and coordinated in public educational television at the University of Wisconsin. Simultaneously she returned to the University of Wisconsin to study Fine Arts in the summers. Soon after this, Mary experienced a spontaneous Soul merging experience, when she came to know her life "via her Soul." Life as artist began and she did not look back.

Biography and Education

Nature was the first potent childhood teacher of Mary Saint-Marie.

Barefoot was her life…running through deep gushing rain in the roadside ditches of Iowa and flying on great vines across ravines of Mississippi and riding great sea turtles on an island in the Gulf of Mexico.

And great was the inspiration of a pioneering pilot mother. Nature provided experiences of a wild oneness…that brought great joy of freedom…later to be captured in painting, writing, sculpting, dancing and sounding.

Formal university education included a degree in Education-English, after which she spent eight years teaching high school and college English, Mythology and Communication. She was also coordinator in public educational TV. Simultaneously Mary studied Fine Art at the University of Wisconsin.

Soon after this Mary had a spontaneous soul merging experience followed shortly by a head-on car collision that provided the opening to see her life *via her soul…as pure joy*. After this Mary could see emanation of light around living things. The exalted experience of the collision initiated a new life. Mary was inspired to begin her life as an artist and to make a solo journey "overland," with a kelty pack filled with one change of clothing and art supplies on her back, to Spain, Morocco, Italy, Greece, Crete, Turkey, Iran, Afghanistan, Pakistan, India and Kashmir, where she felt the art, culture, heart and soul of those peoples.

Upon her return to the U.S., Mary began her first art exhibitions and pioneering shows for mystical and visionary art of the soul. She traveled to wilderness areas for nearly two years, once again feeling the oneness provided by Nature.

Beginning in 1974, Mary has lived mainly in a quiet mountain retreat in Mt. Shasta, California. She is the mother of two grown daughters.

Art, CDs, Soul Sessions, and Soul Retreats

www.MarySaintMarie.com
www.EarthCareGlobalTV.com

Art of the Soul:

All art in *Galactic Shamanism* is available as giclee fine art reproductions.

Inquire to find out if pieces are available as originals.

Please email to find the names of current gallery showings.

*See the website to view videos/youtubes with art.

Books:

Galactic Shamanism
The Sacred Two
The Holy Sight
Nectar of Woman
Messages from the Silence
The Star-Stone Ones
The Animating Presence
The Monitor and Laughter of the Gods, a play in book form
Art As Consciousness
The Oracle and the Dreamer

CDs:

Journey of Consciousness, a meditation
Soul Sounds of World Birth

Recording:

Return to Oneness, a recording giving Voice to the Animals and addressing Rights of Animals (will be made available as a cd)

Soul Sessions and Retreats:

*Please see the website to find out more about the spiritual education for individuals and groups. Mary works both in person and by phone.

Other Sessions, Consultations, and Workshops Available:

Mary's gifts are given as a unique soul expression with each person or group. What comes forth is particular to what is being called forth from the Withinness.

In all of Mary's offerings, one comes to experience:
Mystical AS the Practical
Being the Infinite Beyond Belief
Realization of the Field of Light as Everywhere Present
Awareness of the Divine Feminine Principle, The Great Mother, The Christ of God
Being…Open to the Infinite and FEELing
the embodied Presence

Soul Sessions and Soul Retreats: Being the Infinite

Mary holds sacred space for one's Wholeness. In that Field of Light, one may learn to live from the Soul, the Christ of One's Being.

One may allow Truth of Being to arise.
One may access the Essential Self.
One may behold the Undivided One.
One may feel the Embodied Self.
One may experience the Infinite Love, Intelligence, and Substance of Creation.

Learn to live beyond the sense of separation, beyond beliefs, as an Illumined One.

Learn to experience and feel the Animating Presence, one's Spiritual Identity. This inner Universal Force, this current of Life, is one's Christed Self.

Grace Sessions

For many years, ones have come to me with no problems and with no agendas. These ones are wanting to simply "Sit in Stillness" together…and share of their wonderfully deepening lives in Presence. Often the people in their lives do not understand. This highlights the power of "two or more gathered."

What has been experienced in these sessions is that even more deepening and expansion ensues. Most often new ideas, insights, impulses drop in from the Infinite. These sessions are light-filled.

The Holy Sight

This half to full day workshop teaches one how to realize holy sight (sacred vision) and experience that for oneself and for everyone, everything, and every place.

One's life does change. The Changeless One brings the change.

At the end of workshop, there is an awareness of Holy Sight for the Earth and for the Sky that allows us to hold space for the new Earth emerging.

Learn how to use Christed Spheres of Light to empower one's focus and learn how to let go and surrender, by realizing the Oneness.

Journey of Consciousness: A Meditation

Experience and feel your self as Self. With no sense of separation. Experience your Spiritual Identity, the Soul Self, the God Self, the One Self.

In this extended meditation, one realizes the seeming personal I as the Impersonal I. The experience of Holy Breath, the Light Body, and inner listening are used to experience four subtle and gossamer shifts of consciousness. From a sense of human consciousness, to Divine Consciousness, to I Am Awareness. The rarified air is realized.

Galactic Shamanism: Journey through the Kingdoms and Journey through the Elements

This is a two-day journey into the Oneness with the Earth and Angels and Nature Spirits. It is a way to embrace and live…the Mystical AS the Practical. No separation.

The Voice of Nature Speaks. This is the second part of this workshop. Ones go into Nature to have the inner experience now…in the so-called outer world of Nature.

Initiation into the Ancient Yin-Yang Circle

This is a dedication to the One…come as Man and Woman: The Wedding Ceremony is experienced, as given by White Buffalo Calf Woman. The time is 2–3 hours.

This is a profound experience of the Yin-Yang Balance of man and woman as equal in the emerging new earth culture.

Earth-Sky Heart Initiation

This experience came just after two initiations into the archetypal realms, where Mary had deeper revelations of the emergence of the Divine Feminine on Planet Earth.

It was experienced by Mary just before an upliftment into a realm beyond the human mind. The Realm of Purity of the Blue Kachinas.

This experience allows one to feel deeply the luminous Embodied Self. In Balance. AS Balance.

Sounds and Signings of the Soul

This workshop allows the Soul to reveal the sacred and authentic soul sounds and soul movements. Sounds, Silence, Signings, and Stillness.

One awaits in the Great Emptiness to be animated by Spirit, by the Living Christ of God. In that, one begins to trust the self/Self.

The Sounds of the Soul may come through as soul sounds, songs, chants, drones, or tones.

One begins to "feel" the Universal Force and allow it to express in many ways.

One begins to feel the Oneness with and AS this inner Current of Life. The River of Life.

Sacred Temple Dance

This workshop invites woman to go deeply into the One Self to find and allow Sacred Movements of the Soul. And to allow the power of sacred stances, called Soul Glyphs. These are all positions, postures, gestures, and movements that allow the Inner Power, the current of Life, to be felt. This very Life may then reveal itself as the authentic inner expression of the Self.

It is then that we begin to know the body as The Temple Template of Infinity.

Life as Living Ceremony

This session focusses on leaving prescribed rituals and ceremonies in the past and coming into the realization of…Life as Living Ceremony. Alive, fresh, in the moment, never to be repeated again. The session includes a new way to BE with all aspects of your life.

SHE…it is…Who Remembers

Watch a "sacred enactment of ancient remembering" with narration and living words by Mary Saint-Marie. Feel the Energy of the Arising Feminine in this emerging new culture. Allow one's self/Self to translate what that means in one's own emerging forms of Creation.

Realize the seeming personal I AS the Impersonal I. As Everywhere Present.

I Am the Only Presence Here.
I Am the Only Presence Everywhere.

What does this realization mean in one's own life?
What does life as an Adventure of Awareness look like?

Consultations with Artists and Writers

This consultation is about realizing the Oneness deeply and being animated by it. Mary plays the role of muse, inspiring one's Soul Expression. Mary assists to identify any blocks and reveals how to dissolve them.

Readings: Passages, Parables, and Poetry

Mary's readings of these illumined messages are to facilitate group sharing to rise to seeing with aerial viewing, that is, sight from a higher state of consciousness.

The messages and parables are "passages." They are a passage from one state of consciousness to a higher Consciousness, that life may shape shift into an expression from a higher frequency.

Retreats

Inquire about custom 1–10 day retreats with individuals, groups, businesses, etc.

Mystic/Visionary Art Exhibits

Inquire about exhibitions.

EarthCare Global TV

Please see the website for the full vision of a profound unification of Earth care (www.EarthCareGlobalTV.com).

EarthCare Global TV has as its purpose to freely educate and inspire people of the world about Earth care. It serves to unify ones of like vision through communication and Vision in Action.

EarthCare Global TV sees the understanding of the Universal Law of Balance in all of Nature being shared worldwide that the principle may be realized in daily life by all. The vision shares the practical understanding of the need of purity and sustainability.

*Please see the category, Internet TV, on the website, to see the listing of 280+ Earth care documentaries. The documentaries are about being a Voice for the Earth. And they are education and inspiration for humanity to choose a new direction: Purity instead of pollution.

*See also the category, Videos, on website to view youtubes about the Earth, created with the art of Mary Saint-Marie.

1. *earth care,* a short video created for The One Minute Shift, to expand awareness of the oneness of everyone, everything and everyplace.

2. *Holy Sight for the Earth and for the Sky,* an animation meditation

www.EarthCareGlobalTV.com

Galactic Shamanism is…
when day kisses night…and there is DAWN…
when night kisses day…and there is DUSK…
when past and future merge and…
Ceremony in the NOW…
the Present…
only to present the gift (present)…
of the knowledge of the kingdom of NOW…

www.ingramcontent.com/pod-product-compliance
Lightning Source LLC
Chambersburg PA
CBHW050632160426
43194CB00010B/1640